WALSALL
TROLLEYBUSES
1931–1970

WALSALL TROLLEYBUSES
1931–1970

DAVID HARVEY

AMBERLEY

Amberley Publishing
Cirencester Road, Chalford,
Stroud, Gloucestershire, GL6 8PE

British Library Cataloguing in Publication Data.
A catalogue record for this book is available from the British Library.

ISBN 978-1-84868-464-5

Typesetting and origination by Amberley Publishing
Printed in Great Britain

CONTENTS

PREFACE

This book examines the development, expansion and eventual decline of this, the smallest of the three West Midlands municipal trolleybus operators. The Walsall system was interesting in that it had over twenty years of stability but with the arrival of a new general manager the size of the operation doubled in size. Each route has been examined in detail by taking a journey along every one of them from either Walsall town centre or from the nucleus of the northern extension in Bloxwich. Each chapter looks at a selection of the trolleybuses used on the route over time and the areas through which the route travelled. Enjoy the trip around the efficient and always interesting Walsall system in the middle years of the twentieth century when trolleybuses were an integral part of the town's public transport scene.

David Harvey
Dudley
June 2009

HISTORY

Walsall Corporation began operating tramcars on the standard 3ft 6in gauge tracks on New Year's Day January 1904 and its first buses in May 1915. Powers to operate trolleybuses in Walsall were first obtained in the Walsall Corporation Act of 1914 which authorised routes from Rushall to Walsall Wood and from Bloxwich to Hednesford by way of Cannock. There was also a proposal to build from the tram terminus to Newton Road. All of these trolleybus, or 'railless', routes were extensions of the existing tram routes. The Walsall Corporation Act of 1925 gave the municipality the powers to operate trolleybuses on any existing tram routes within the Borough and beyond the Borough boundaries to Willenhall, Walsall Wood and Brownhills.

The first tram route to be replaced was that to Walsall Wood on 1 April 1928, but despite trolleybus operating powers the route was converted to motorbus operation using a fleet of the somewhat rare Dennis H type double-deckers. The second tram route to be replaced was the Birmingham Road route in September 1928; this had at one time been supposed to be extended to the Scott Arms at Great Barr, but nothing came of it.

The pioneering trolleybus conversions introduced by Mr C. Owen Silvers in neighbouring Wolverhampton now began to influence the next conversion. Wolverhampton had introduced trolleybuses as early as 29 October 1923 when the Wednesfield route was converted to trolleybus operation, and such was the success of these vehicles that a fairly rapid conversion programme was undertaken in the town. The Wolverhampton Corporation single-deck trams to Willenhall were converted to trolleybus operation over several months with single-deck trolleybuses reaching Willenhall's Market Place on 16 September 1927.

William Vane Morland was appointed as general manager in 1926 and was an advocate of motorbus operation and a pioneer of operating buses with heavy oil engines. He was given the task of running down the municipal tram fleet, but it was perhaps surprising that he presided, for the only time in his career, over the introduction of a trolleybus route. An interesting aside was that he is a fine amateur actor who regularly appeared in leading parts of Shakespearian roles for the Walsall Players.

An agreement to operate a joint trolleybus service was reached after Walsall had closed down the Walsall-Willenhall tram route on 3 February 1929 and a jointly operated bus service between Walsall, Willenhall and Wolverhampton was successfully substituted. Initially Walsall Corporation was reluctant to begin trolleybus operations, and it was encouraged to do so by the desire of its near neighbour at Wolverhampton to have through running between the two towns by this still fairly new method of public transport. It was decided that the joint trolleybus service should be operated by double-deck vehicles, but through working could not be completed until road alterations had been completed in Horseley Fields.

Walsall required just four trolleybuses for the initial service to Willenhall and so two AEC 663Ts and two Guy BTXs were acquired becoming the only trolleybuses chassis Walsall ever operated by these two manufacturers. These four sixty-seat vehicles were purchased in order to operate the route to Willenhall with the intention of linking up with the Wolverhampton trolleybuses to form an interurban service between the two towns. The original route to Willenhall was opened on 22 July 1931 and numbered 28. Wolverhampton's shortworkings as far as Willenhall were given the route number 5. The through working between Walsall and Wolverhampton of jointly operated service began on 16 November 1931 after the road works lowering the carriageway beneath the railway bridge at Horseley Fields were completed enabling double-deckers of both Corporations to reach Wolverhampton town centre. The through working by both municipal operators was given the route number 29.

On 30 September 1930, the last tram services operated by the South Staffordshire Tramways Company, the dying giant of electric tramway operation in the Black Country, from Wednesbury to Darlaston, Wednesbury to the Walsall boundary at James Bridge and Darlaston to James Bridge were transferred to Walsall Corporation. On the following day the Corporation took over operation of what was effectively operated as a circular service until this too was abandoned on 4 April 1931. This left Walsall Corporation as the last operator of trams in the area working on the Bloxwich service.

The appointment of Mr M. J. Somerfield as the new general manager in April 1932 coincided with the increasing need to replace the last Corporation tram route. The second trolleybus service to Bloxwich (route 30), replaced the Corporation's trams. The introduction of trolleybuses on this route was due to the track on the very busy Bloxwich tram route nearing the end of its life and it was not considered economical to renew the track. In some ways this was surprising as the last ten open balcony, four-wheel trams, 40-49, had only been built by Brush in 1920 and the preceding batch of UEC-bodied cars numbered 33-39 had only been built in 1912. Despite the age and excellent condition of these remaining tramcars, the decision to convert this, the final tram route in the town, was made. As Birchills depot in Bloxwich Road was already wired up for the Wolverhampton service and the depot was about half way between Walsall town centre and Bloxwich, the added cost of altering the electrical infrastructure must have played an important part in the decision to abandon the trams.

A ceremony was held on Friday 29 September 1933 to inaugurate the service officially and the last Bloxwich trams ran on 30 September 1933. Normal trolleybus operation began at 10am on 1 October 1933. They used fifteen brand new Sunbeam MS2 six-wheelers with fleet numbers 155-169. Beadle, Short and Weymann each supplied five bodies as part of this contract

In 1937, a proposal to convert the motorbus circular service linking Walsall, Wednesbury and Darlaston to trolleybus operation was made. The anti-clockwise No. 37 circular service to Walsall-Pleck-Wednesbury-Darlaston-Pleck-Walsall and the clockwise No. 38 Walsall-Pleck-Darlaston-Wednesbury-Pleck-Walsall route was the intended conversion but the failure of Wednesbury Corporation to agree to the scheme led to the advanced planning being abandoned.

In 1938 another two Sunbeam MS2 six-wheelers were purchased only this time with Park Royal bodies, while in 1940 another four basically identical vehicles were purchased. Thus by March 1940, the Walsall trolleybus fleet numbered twenty-five vehicles.

Although there were no further route extensions during the Second World War, the Ministry of War Transport allocated twelve of the standard issue of Sunbeam W4 trolleybuses to Walsall because of increased traffic requirements. These trolleybuses had the fixty-six-seat 'utility' bodywork contracts divided between Park Royal, Brush or Roe. The twelve wartime acquisitions purchased between 1943 and 1946 were all two-axle vehicles because the Sunbeam/Karrier W4 four-wheelers were the only type of trolleybus made available through the Ministry of War Transport. Yet their operation caused a change in Walsall's post-war trolleybus purchasing policy so that, with one exception, all future trolleybuses would be two-axled rather than the pre-war standard of three-axled vehicles.

Two unusual trolleybuses were operated on loan by Walsall between June 1943 and either July or August 1945. These were twin door and staircase English Electric-bodied Sunbeam MS2s owned by Bournemouth Corporation, although they had come directly from a period of loan with South Shields Corporation. The four original trolleybuses purchased in 1931 for the Willenhall service were withdrawn in 1945 and 1946. The delivery of the last wartime trolleybuses arrived in March 1946 and for the next four years the system enjoyed a period of stability. During 1947, the original type of trolley head wheels were replaced by carbon slipper gear which reduced dewirements and was much quieter, though many people missed the swoosh of the approaching trolleybus. At the end of 1949 an order was placed for ten new Sunbeam F4 four-wheel trolleybuses with Brush composite bodywork. In October 1950, all the surviving pre-war six-wheelers and all the wartime 'Utility'-bodied Sunbeam W4s were renumbered in a continuous new series with the original 155 becoming 301 and 237 becoming 333.

The terminus in Park Street for the Walsall-Wolverhampton joint service was moved from its former prominent position to a more convenient, yet somewhat skulking location behind the Savoy Cinema in Townend Street. Meanwhile, the second route to Bloxwich still used the impressively sited terminus at The Bridge, but the inward journey was made by way of St Paul's Street rather than from Park Street. For the time being the outward journey still went northwards along Park Street into Stafford Street where it met the inbound vehicles working on the No. 30 route. All of the NDH-registered trolleybuses were in service by the November 1951 thus eliminating the ten Sunbeam MS2s with Beadle and Short-bodied of 1933.

Walsall's interest in trolleybuses only really expanded in the 1950s after the appointment of Mr Ronald Edgley Cox as the Corporation's general manager on 1 June 1952. During his seventeen year tenure, the size of the trolleybus fleet increased from thirty-four vehicles to sixty-nine in order to cope with the introduction of new trolleybus routes to the north of the town. In the late 1950s and into the 1960s new routes were opened to the north of the town centre. The first of these was the circular service to Blakenall, opened on 6 June 1955, with the No. 15 route going anti-clockwise off Bloxwich Lane via Coalpool Lane, Harden Road and into Bloxwich from Lichfield Road, while the clockwise No. 30 service went directly to Bloxwich along Bloxwich Road before returning via Blakenall.

The Stephenson Avenue, Leamore via Cavendish Avenue to Sneyd Hall Road, Dudley Fields No. 33 route was opened on 12 September 1955. On 1 November 1961 the No. 33 route was extended into Bloxwich creating another circular route. A branch along Bloxwich Lane to the junction in Cavendish Road in Leamore was introduced on 2 September 1963 becoming the last route extension to open. A further extension along Cavendish Road back to Stevenson Avenue was envisaged but never constructed.

The No. 31 route was introduced on 3 June 1957 and went out of the town centre along Bloxwich Road where it passed Walsall Corporation's Birchills garage and works. On reaching Bloxwich the No. 31 route turned left into Wolverhampton Road, Bell Lane and Sneyd Lane and the turning right into Cresswell Crescent before terminating at Abbey Square. On 20 September 1959 the route was extended to the Eagle Hotel in Cresswell Crescent just short of Broad Lane at the Walsall-Staffordshire boundary.

The penultimate trolleybus route to open was the No. 32 service which turned right into Park Road and Lichfield Road at the northern end of Bloxwich before turning left into Stoney Lane, reaching the Lower Farm Estate terminus at Buxton Road on 31 December 1962.

Had not Wolverhampton's trolleybus policy dramatically changed in June 1957, almost on the same day as the Mossley trolleybus route was opened, an even more interesting trolleybus route might have been opened. A proposal around the time of the Suez Crisis was made to extend the Wolverhampton No. 9 service from the Pheasant public house in Wood End Road to the Albion public house on Lichfield Road, Wednesfield using Linthouse Lane. This would have created a circular service using the No. 59 route number. As a result of this suggestion and Mr Edgley Cox's wish to enlarge the Walsall system, a tentative proposition was made to link the 2-mile gap between the Albion terminus on the main A4124 Lichfield Road with Walsall's No. 31 Mossley service where Lichfield Road becomes Sneyd Lane in Bloxwich. Unfortunately, nothing came of the Wednesfield extension and this second inter-urban route was stillborn. But this only tells part of the story; the rest of the fascinating history, the vehicles and the routes and services are found in the photographic record of this book.

During his long term at Birchills, which began in 1952, R. E. Cox's motorbus policy was to purchase anything that was innovative, new or unusual, always in 'penny' numbers, and then for the next purchase obtain something totally different. However, his trolleybus purchasing policy was at first very different. Initially he ordered a solitary twin-staircase trolleybus equipped for a seated conductor and 'pay-as-you-board' facilities (the only post-war six-wheel vehicle to be purchased). Then in 1954 his ordering of twenty-two new trolleybuses broke the archaic regulations, which led to the introduction for the first time in the UK of a 30ft long double-decker bus on two, not three, axles. As a result, over a period of two years twenty-two Willowbrook-bodied Sunbeam F4As were delivered.

In preparation for the opening of a new trolleybus service to Blakenall in 1955, Walsall purchased fifteen F4A trolleybuses with Willowbrook bodywork which entered service between November 1954 and June 1955. A second batch of seven similar trolleybuses went on the road between June and October 1956 for the opening of a new trolleybus service to Beechdale and also to replace some of the early three-axle trolleybuses. Special permission had to be obtained to operate these vehicles because they were 30ft long on a two-axle chassis and therefore the first trolleybuses to be built to these specifications. No. 872 was the highest numbered vehicle in the second batch and on 14 October 1956 became the last new trolleybus of all to enter service with Walsall. Until the closure of the system they were the backbone of the Walsall trolleybus fleet being used on the Bloxwich group of services.

Yet it was the dabbling in the second-hand trolleybus market that gave the Walsall system its interest. Two trolleybuses were purchased from Pontypridd UDC in 1956 while in 1959 eight former Hastings Tramways vehicles were purchased. These and the eight former Ipswich trolleybuses bought in 1962 all had 95 hp motors, and because of their better performance they were used on the joint Walsall-Wolverhampton service almost exclusively until the closure of that route in 1965. Between these two batches of buses two quite rare Crossley trolleybuses and four BUT 9611Ts from Grimsby-Cleethorpes were purchased, bringing the trolleybus fleet up to its maximum size of sixty-one vehicles.

Although the Wolverhampton system was well on the way to being closed down, the first Walsall trolleybus route to close was the jointly operated No. 29 service. This was due to the construction of the M6 motorway which passed through Bentley. Work began on this extensive civil engineering scheme in 1963 and although the No. 29 route soldiered on for over two years eventually building restrictions became so bad that this jointly operated trolleybus service was closed on 31 October 1965.

The trolleybus system's terminal decline and a nod to the inevitable began when Sunday operation of trolleybuses ended on 10 March 1968. Despite this, Mr Cox prepared an outline for a 35ft long two-axle 100-seater one-man-operated double-deck trolleybus with 3 doors and 2 staircases; it never got beyond the drawing board. Yet a version of this of design did appear in 1968 as the solitary 56, (XDH 56G), a Daimler 'Fleetline' CRC6-30 motorbus fitted with a Northern Counties H51/35D body.

A further experiment involved one of the pair of Crossley TDD42/3s. 873, (HBE 542), was taken out of service and experimentally fitted with an oil engine beneath the staircase, though it never ran in this condition. At the very end of his tenure, in January 1969, Mr Edgley Cox had on loan Bournemouth's 300, (300 LJ), a Sunbeam MF2B with a Weymann H37/28D bodywork which dated from September 1962. Modifications were made on this bus by fitting a small auxiliary Diesel engine mounted beneath the rear staircase in order that it could operate away from overhead power lines in a manner common throughout Europe. If this experiment had been successful the proposal was to purchase the remaining thirty-eight Bournemouth Corporation Sunbeam MF2B trolleybuses, which were only between seven and ten years old, and similarly convert them to a bi-modal Diesel-electric arrangement. The front entrance was to be widened and the open rear platform and rear staircase removed. The interest in these Bournemouth vehicles was because of the need for extra trolleybuses to serve on five proposed route extensions.

As late as 1969, a Parliamentary Bill was seeking provision for five additional links between existing routes. These would have included the extension along Cavendish Road back to Stephenson Avenue, although by this time the planned Bloxwich Lane extension to link with the Wolverhampton joint service had been superseded by the closure of the No. 29 route due to the M6 civil engineering works. A new route along Green Lane to Bloxwich by way of the Four Crosses and Somerfield Road was proposed which would have intersected with a route following Leamore Lane across Green Lane and Bloxwich Road before linking with the No. 15/30 route at The Royal Oak junction at the eastern end of Harden Road. There was intended to be a link from Blakenall church through the 'village' along Blakenall Lane to Bloxwich Road at Leamore and going in the opposite direction from Blakenall along Green Rock Lane and Livingstone Road to Lichfield Road, Little Bloxwich, just east of where the Lower Farm No. 31 route turned off the A4124. Finally the short section of Bell Lane from the terminus of the Bloxwich services at the junction with Lichfield Road to Wolverhampton Road was also proposed.

By the late 1960s Walsall Corporation's trolleybus fleet had become the home of redundant trolleybuses from elsewhere in the country. Just as in Bradford, enthusiasts would flock to see this quite small but efficient system encouraged by the purchasing policy of their general manager, Ronald Edgley Cox, who from the late 1950s was dipping into the second-hand trolleybus market as operators began to abandon their systems. The Walsall trolleybus system, despite being a successful operation and being quite unique in the area, had become something of an anachronism and was therefore an early target for replacement. The Corporation was, right up to the last months of its independence, an enthusiastic proponent of trolleybuses. This was despite the Walsall trolleybus fleet being the only surviving one to be taken over by any of the Passenger Transport Authorities when West Midlands PTE took-over the municipal bus operation on 1 October 1969.

On 6 February 1970 the system began to be closed down when the entire Acocks Green fleet of former Birmingham Corporation Guy 'Arab' III Specials were drafted into Birchills. Although no routes were withdrawn and the trolleybus mileage remained the same, all the former Hastings Tramways trolleybuses and all but one of the Ipswich vehicles were taken out of service. The replacement motorbuses were used on the trolleybus routes and were frequently interspersed with the electric fleet.

Walsall's mechanical and electrical acumen was rather masked by their fleet's diversity. In later years, the impression was of a fleet of vehicles, in their contradictory dull-all-over bright blue livery that was shabby and unloved, yet the condition of the overhead and general infrastructure was always excellent. Undoubtedly, Walsall Corporation did have its detractors. The hard-pressed fleet usually looked in need of a repaint, while the lack of standardisation must have been a considerable headache for the mechanical staff. Yet there was a certain air of expectancy about the town's public transport system as for a time there was almost something different each month! Historically, quite late trolleybus route extensions, forays into the second-hand trolleybus market to fund these new extensions and the rebuilding of some of these acquired vehicles with almost new, home-made bodies always made the idiosyncratic Walsall system look interesting. But underneath all this was an undertaking that made a profit.

Let us make a visit back in time to Walsall and the surrounding area as it was and take a journey by trolleybus from the beginnings of the operation on 16 November 1931 until it was closed for normal operation on Friday 2 October 1970 by West Midland PTE. The following morning a special service between St

Paul's Bus Station and Bloxwich was operated using one trolleybus from each of the surviving types. 342, the lengthened Sunbeam F4, ex-Ipswich 353, 'Liner' 859 and the forward entrance 875 were used throughout the Sunday. Enthusiasts, local folk and ordinary passengers – unaware that this was the last day and therefore not happy to be charged one shilling and still be 'turfed-off' at Bloxwich – all rode on these trolleybuses up and down Bloxwich Road.

As darkness came, the final three trolleybuses – 862, later to go to the Black Country Museum; 864, to be preserved by the National Trolleybus Association; and the illuminated 872, driven by Mr Edgley Cox himself – left Birchills for the last time going first to Bloxwich, then back along Bloxwich Road to St Paul's Bus Station before returning to the garage for the last time.

GENERAL MANAGERS

R. L. Horsfield	1903–1920
C. Burgess	1920–1926
W. Vane Morland	1926–1932
M. J. Somerfield	1932–1952
R. Edgley Cox	1952–1969

WALSALL TROLLEYBUS DESTINATION ROUTES

15. WALSALL—BLAKENALL—BLOXWICH—LEAMORE—WALSALL (Circular)
15. WALSALL—BLAKENALL (Shortworking)
28. WALSALL—WILLENHALL
29. WALSALL—WILLENHALL—WOLVERHAMPTON (Joint with Wolverhampton)
30. WALSALL—LEAMORE—BLOXWICH—BLAKENALL—WALSALL (Circular)
31. WALSALL—LEAMORE—BLOXWICH—MOSSLEY ESTATE
32. WALSALL—LEAMORE—BLOXWICH—LOWER FARM ESTATE
33. WALSALL—LEAMORE—BLOXWICH—CAVENDISH ROAD—BEECHDALE ESTATE—WALSALL
34. WALSALL—LEAMORE (Shortworking)
40. WALSALL—GIPSY LANE—BEECHDALE ESTATE

Trolleybus Routes

1. Willenhall opened 22 July 1931 as the No. 29 ROUTE and opened as a joint route to Wolverhampton on 16 November 1931. Closed 31 October 1965. *c. 6.2 miles*

2. Bloxwich (No. 30 ROUTE) replaced the last Corporation's trams on 1 October 1933. Closed 3 October 1970. *c. 3.0 miles*

3. Walsall-Blakenall opened on 6 June 1955 as the No. 15 ROUTE. Extended to Bloxwich on 10 October 1955 with No. 15 ROUTE ANTI-CLOCKWISE AND No. 30 ROUTE CLOCKWISE. Closed 2 October 1970. *c. 3.2 miles*

4. Green Lane and Stephenson Avenue, Leamore to Beechdale Estate, was opened on 12 September 1955 as the No. 40 ROUTE. Closed 2 September 1963. *c. 2.0 miles*

5. Walsall, Bloxwich, Bell Lane, Sneyd Lane and Cresswell Crescent (Abbey Square), Mossley (No. 31 ROUTE). Introduced on 3 June 1957. Closed 20 September 1959. *c. 0.7 miles*. On 20 September 1959 the route was extended to the Eagle Hotel in Cresswell Crescent, Mossley. Closed 2 October 1970. *c. 0.3 miles*

6. Walsall, Bloxwich, Park Road, Lichfield Road, Stoney Lane to Buxton Road on the Lower Farm Estate. Introduced on 31 December 1962, this was the penultimate trolleybus service to open and was NUMBERED ROUTE 32. Closed 2 October 1970. *c. 1.1 miles*

7. The No. 33 ROUTE was EXTENDED to Sneyd Hall Road, Dudley Fields INTO Bloxwich via as a circular service on 1 November 1961. Closed 2 October 1970. *c. 2.6 miles*. A branch of the No. 33 ROUTE along Bloxwich Lane to the junction in Cavendish Road in Leamore was introduced on 2 September 1963. Closed 2 October 1970. *c. 0.5 miles*

This was the last route extension to open whereupon the Walsall trolleybus system reached its maximum mileage of *18.86*.

WALSALL TROLLEYBUS FLEET

Fleet No	Reg. No	Chassis	Chassis No	Motors	Body	Body No	Seating Capacity	In Service	Out of Service
151-152	DH 8311-2	AEC 663T	663T004-5	EE 80hp	English Electric		H32/28R	7/31	1-2/46
153-154	DH 8313-4	Guy BTX	BTX 23641/39	Rees-Roturbo 60hp	Brush		H32/28R	7/31	9/45
155-159 (301-305)	ADH 1-5	Sunbeam MS2	12010/2/4 /3/5	MV BTH 80hp	Beadle	299-300 /2/1/3	H32/28R	10/33 155 8/33	1-9/51
160-164 (306-310)	ADH 6-10	Sunbeam MS2	12016/1 /7-9	MV BTH 80hp	Short		H32/28R	10/33 164 8/33	9-10/51
165-169 (311-315)	ADH 11-15	Sunbeam MS2	12009/20-3	MV BTH 80hp	Weymann	C540-44	H32/28R	10/33 167 8/33	2/55 (312) 9/56
187-88 (316-317)	EDH 863-864	Sunbeam MS2	121150-1	MV BTH 80hp	Park Royal	B4925-6	H32/28R	2/38	7-8/56
216-219 (318-321)	HDH 211-214	Sunbeam MS2	12225-8	MV 80hp	Park Royal	B5791-4	H32/28R	2-3/40	8-9/56
225-226 (322-323)	JDH 29-30	Sunbeam W4	50029-30	MV BTH 85hp	Park Royal	B17926-7	UH30/26R	8/43	12/59, 1/61
Bournemouth CT 78-79	AEL 406-407	Sunbeam MS2	12030-33S	MV BTH 80 hp	English Electric		H31/25D	6-7/34	ON LOAN 1/6/43- (78) 22/8/45, 17/7/45
228-230 (324-326)	JDH 331-333	Sunbeam W4	50147-9	MV BTH 85hp	Brush		UH30/26R	5-6/45	9-10/59
231-232 (327-328)	JDH 339-340	Sunbeam W4	50157/6	MV BTH 85hp	Park Royal	B29206-7	UH30/26R	8/45	4/60/ (327) 5/65

Fleet No	Reg. No	Chassis	Chassis No	Motors	Body	Body No	Seating capacity	In service	Out of service
233 (329)	JDH 334	Sunbeam W4	50150	MV BTH 85hp	Brush		UH30/26R	6/45	6/64
234-237 (330-333)	JDH 430/2-4	Sunbeam W4	50293-6	MV BTH 85hp	Roe	GO2086/3-5	UH30/26R	2-3/46	12/65 234 11/62
334-343	NDH951-960	Sunbeam F4	50732-41	MV BTH 95hp	Brush		H30/26R	12/50 (334) 10-11/51	11/64-12/67 ToWMPTE 10/69
342					Reb. to 30' 5/65		H34/31R		338-42 7-10/70
850 (350)	RDH 990	Sunbeam S7	70031	MV BTH 115hp	Willowbrook	53107	H38/24D H36/7RD (2/61)	9/53	5/67
DEMO FROM GLASGOW CT TBS 2	FYS 766	BUT RETB1	521590	EE 120hp	East Lancs	4890	B27D	2/53	ON LOAN 19/2-16/3/53
851-865	TDH 901-915	Sunbeam F4A	9022-3/5/4/6/8-9/7/33/6/30-2/5/4	MV BTH 95hp	Willowbrook	54172-85	H36/34RD	11/54-6/55	To WMPTE 10/69 3/70, (856) 10/70 (852-5/7-65)
EX-PONTYPRIDD UDC 14-15 12/1955 301-302	FTG 697-698	Karrier W4	50312-3	MV BTH 85hp	Roe	GO2089-90	UH30/26R	3/46	2/62-1/63
866-872	XDH 66-72	Sunbeam F4A	9037-43	MV BTH 95hp	Willowbrook	557701-7	H36/34RD	6/56-10/56	To WMPTE 10/69, 3/70 (871) 10/70 (866-70/2)
866					Reb.6/69		H37/34F		

Fleet No	Reg. No	Chassis	Chassis No	Motors	Body	Body No	Seating capacity	In service	Out of service
Ex-Hastings Tramways 31/3/6-9/41/4 6-7/1959 303-310	BDY 806/8/11 -14/6/9	Sunbeam W4	50432/4/7- 40/2/5	MV BTH 95hp	Weymann	9152/8/ 61/55/3/ 60/4/54	H30/26R	8/47-8/48	11/65 (305) To WMPTE 10/69 2/70
Ex-Grimsby—Cleethorpes 159-162 7/1960 874-877	GFU 692-5	BUT 9611T	9611T 131-4	MV 115hp	NCB		H28/26R	7-9/50	To WMPTE 10/69 2/70 (874) 3/70 (877) 10/70 (875-6)
875-877					Reb. to 30' 1/62- 7/63		H39/30F (875-6) H37/30F (877)		
Ex-Grimsby—Cleethorpes 163-4, 7/1960 850/873	HBE 541-2	Crossley TDD42 /3	94444-5	MV 95hp	Roe	GO3288 /7	H29/25R	2/51	12/67 (873) To WMPTE 10/69 2/70
873					Reb. with oil engine -/68				
Ex-Ipswich 119-126 2-5/1962 344-347/ 351-354	ADX 193-196/ 189-192	Sunbeam F4	50677-80/ 50673-6	MV 95hp	Park Royal	B33261- 4/57-60	H30/26R	7/50	2/66 (354) To WMPTE 10/69 2/70 (344-7/51-2) 10/70 (353)
Bournemouth CT 300 300	300 LJ	Sunbeam MF2B	TFD 80201		Weymann Reb. with oil engine	M9521	H37/28D	9/62	ON LOAN 1/69-8/69

CHAPTER ONE

WOLVERHAMPTON JOINT SERVICE

There were fifty trolleybus systems in the United Kingdom, but there were only eight examples of joint operation of trolleybuses. The examples from around the country were between Ashton-under-Lyne and Oldham Corporations, (August 1925 to September 1926); Ashton, again, with Manchester Corporation, (March 1938 to December 1966); Brighton Corporation and Brighton, Hove and District, (April 1939 to March 1959); Grimsby Corporation and Cleethorpes Corporation, (July 1937 to June 1960); Mexborough and Swinton, a B.E.T. Company; and Rotherham Corporation, (March 1929 to March 1961). Finally there was South Lancashire Transport and St Helens Corporation, (June 1931 to November 1956). Though not strictly a joint working, the Nottinghamshire and Derbyshire Traction Company ran under Nottingham Corporation wiring for some 3 miles along Nottingham Road from October 1933 until April 1953.

In the West Midlands the only example of jointly operated trolleybuses was the 29 service between Walsall and Wolverhampton via Bentley and Willenhall. Wolverhampton Corporation had opened the trolleybus service on 16 September 1927, as far as the famous lock-making town of Willenhall. This marked the limit of Wolverhampton's operational boundary. After the failure to agree with the adjacent Corporation about the extension of the new trolleybus service into Walsall, a jointly operated single-deck motorbus service began on 4 February 1929. This was the day after Walsall Corporation had closed its tram route to Willenhall. Walsall was reluctant to invest in the infrastructure required for trolleybus operation. It had been agreed that if the receipts warranted it, Walsall would convert the route to trolleybus operation, providing that the road was lowered beneath the low LNWR/LMS railway bridge in Horseley Fields, just outside Wolverhampton town centre to enable double-deckers to pass through. The Wolverhampton Corporation single-deck trolleybus service was suspended on 27 April 1931, initially for the bridge over the Wolverhampton level of the Birmingham Canal to be strengthened and then to lower the road beneath the railway bridge. These road works were completed in mid-September 1931, but Wolverhampton continued to operate their single-decker trolleybuses until the overhead was wired for double-deckers.

Meanwhile, Walsall opened its first trolleybus route to Willenhall on 22 July 1931. The new route, numbered 29, started from Townend at the top end of Park Street beyond the railway station. This was a bustling area of small shops, warehouses and back street workshops and until 1950 trolleybuses turned around at the top of Park Street until the loop around the ABC Cinema was introduced. The joint working of double-deck trolleybuses between Walsall and Wolverhampton began on Monday 6 November 1931. This was the route for which the Corporation purchased four six-wheel double-deck trolleybuses. These were two English Electric-bodied AEC 663Ts and two Brush-bodied Guy BTXs. No other pre-war trolleybuses with either of these chassis or body manufacturers' products were operated by Walsall again.

The electricity for the joint service was supplied by Wolverhampton Corporation as far as Willenhall Market Place, and the turning wires at the traffic island at the bottom of Rose Hill where coincidentally the Wolverhampton interurban 25 route from Fighting Cocks via Bilston terminated. Walsall trolleybuses turning back at the Market Place, Willenhall were charged a levy of 2s 6d per 100 workings. Willenhall was the only turn back point on the jointly operated service and was given the route number 5.

The joint service was extremely successful, but after 1950 the Walsall terminus was taken out of the Townend/Park Street turning circle and the trolleybuses used Green Lane, Townend Street and Wolverhampton Street as a new terminal loop around the ABC Cinema. Similar problems with congestion at the junction of Pipers Row and Horseley Fields end of the No. 29 route led to a new terminus being brought into use on 15 October 1951 using St James's Square in Wolverhampton.

Throughout the 1950s the Walsall share of the 29 route was operated by the wartime fleet of Sunbeam W4s and the 1951 batch of 95 hp Brush-bodied Sunbeam F4s, but by the end of the decade even Walsall's ingenious bodybuilders were struggling to keep the 'Utility'-bodied vehicles roadworthy. In 1959, Mr Cox took one of his earliest forays into the second-hand trolleybus market and purchased eight former Hastings Tramways trolleybuses from Maidstone and District who had taken over the Hastings system and then promptly closed it down. In 1962 another eight vehicles were purchased, this time from Ipswich Corporation. Both of these second-hand batches had 95 hp motors, matching the power output of the indigenous NDH-registered batch and these sixteen trolleybuses almost exclusively began to operate the 29 service, nominally replacing the ex-Hastings vehicles on the route, although in practice both types were used side-by-side.

By the early 1960s the pendulum had swung totally around and it was at the insistence of Walsall Corporation that the joint service would remain operated by trolleybuses until at least 1967. From 1963 the joint service was left virtually unaltered until Wolverhampton took the decision to begin to close down the trolleybus system in the town. However, the national needs for a motorway linking the Midlands to the North-West, rather overtook the fortunes of a solitary trolleybus route and after much wrangling over the proposed route, construction of the new motorway began in 1963. It cut across the trolleybus route at Bentley, destroying Bentley Hall at the same time. Eventually, because of the construction of the M6 motorway at Bentley, the trolleybus service closed on 31 October 1965. The replacement bus service retained the number 29 and used the same service loop around the ABC Cinema as the trolleybuses.

In order to cover this route fully from Walsall to Wolverhampton via Willenhall and to show how much it has changed, there are photographs of trolleybuses and the replacement buses belonging to both Walsall and Wolverhampton Corporations.

Turning out of Wolverhampton Street in front of Her Majesty's Theatre at the Townend Bank turning loop at the junction with Park Street in 1936 is Walsall's first trolleybus. No. 151, (DH 8313), was originally going to be numbered 7. This AEC 663T was fitted with an English Electric H32/28R and was one of a pair delivered in July 1931 for the opening of the service on 22 July of the same year. Her Majesty's Theatre at Townend Bank was opened in March 1900. It was designed by Owen & Ward and could hold up to 2,000 people. It became a variety theatre in 1905, was converted into a cinema in 1933 and was demolished in 1937. In 1938 the Savoy Cinema, later the ABC, was opened on the site.

(R. T. Wilson)

The Savoy Cinema dominated the open space opposite the Park Street junction. To the left, from where the Wolverhampton Corporation has come from, is Wolverhampton Street, while to the right is Green Lane where the traction poles have already been put into position for the repositioning of the 29 terminus alongside the rear of the Savoy Cinema. 650, (FJW 650), a Guy BT with a Park Royal H28/26R body is one of Wolverhampton's last trolleybuses, having entered service on 30 March 1950. It is turning around in the wide-open space to pull up outside the Warwickshire Furniture Company's shop just above the impressive wood-fronted Red Lion public house (built in 1896) at the top of Park Street. Hidden by the trolleybus is Stafford Street, which is the road by which the Bloxwich route left the town centre.

(J. S. Webb)

The first Walsall trolleybus, 151, (DH 8311), was this AEC 663T powered by an English Electric 80hp motor and fitted with a five-bay English Electric H33/27R body. The bodies fitted to 151 and 152 were very similar to three constructed in 1930 at the Dick, Kerr Works in Preston and fitted to the first three AEC 663Ts to be built. These three trolleybuses were HX 1460, which was demonstrated to London United and actually operated in Nottingham; an unregistered demonstrator to Birmingham, which was rechassied and with a Brush body became BCT's 16, (OJ 1016); and finally LJ 7702, which eventually became Bournemouth 69. These were all used as demonstrators but because their bodies were quickly seen to be structurally weak all were taken out of service and re-bodied and/or rebuilt. This pair for Walsall had the next chassis numbers of 663T004 and 005 and were the only ones of the first five to survive with this original style of five-bay English Electric body. The trolleybus is loading up in Park Street shortly after the 29 route's introduction in November 1931. The trolleybus is displaying an advertisement for the locally brewed Highgate Mild Ales, based in Sandymount Road, Walsall since 1899 and, despite changing hands on several occasions, is today a thriving independent brewer.

(D. R. Harvey Collection)

The second of the pair of trolleybuses was originally going to be numbered 8, but it entered service as No. 152, (DH 8312). It is standing at the top of Park Street almost in front of the Red Lion public house built in 1896, which survives today as a real gem of Victorian pub architecture. Townend was never an area occupied by 'town centre' type shops but had the advantage of the large open area in front of the Her Majesty's Theatre that allowed the inbound trolleybuses from Wolverhampton to turn round. In the background are the rows of early nineteenth-century premises in Park Street. The 29 route was opened on Monday 16 November 1931 and No. 152 is working on the route shortly after this date. These AEC 663Ts had attractive-looking English Electric H33/27R bodies which had the lower saloon ventilators mounted at cant-rail level, suggesting that the lower saloon ceilings were not curved at the outer edges. The front design did belong to a period between 1930 and about 1934 when the frontal design of the trolleybuses was frequently uncertain with rounded cowls, dummy radiators or, as in this case, a plethora of ventilation slots.

(D. R. Harvey Collection)

The crew of the Weymann-bodied Sunbeam MS2 relax alongside the cab of their trolleybus. The vehicle No. 167, (ADH 13), is standing at the second terminus at Townend which was on the northern side of Marsh Street about 100yds away from the initial one. It is still quite new as it still has the original elaborately lined-out livery. The trolleybus is working on the No. 29 service but the crew have yet to change the destination blind round to show Wolverhampton in readiness for the return journey.

(D. R. Harvey Collection)

Shortly after being renumbered as 323 in 1950, Park Royal-bodied Sunbeam W4, the former No. 226 is parked just above the Warwickshire Furniture Company in Wolverhampton Street alongside The Dun Cow public house. This town centre hostelry was owned by William Butlers & Co. and was opened in 1905 and closed in 1961. Behind the trolleybus coming out of Marsh Street is a 1949 Commer van based on a Hillman Minx saloon car. Working on the shortworking to Willenhall, No. 323 was the first wartime trolleybus to enter service on 21 August 1943 and would survive until January 1961.

(A. B. Cross)

Throughout most of West Midlands PTE operations, the Walsall terminus of the No. 529 route was at the top of Park Street outside the Boots the Chemists store. In 1985, WM's 4677, (GOG 677N), one of the short-lived Bristol VRT/SL6Gs with MCW H43/33F bodies waits in the summer sunshine carrying an advertisement for Weetabix which coincidentally is also being advertised on the bus stop. No. 4677 was a Walsall bus and because both Birchills and Cleveland Road garages operated these Bristol VRs, it was the only route in the North Division that drivers' rotas enabled them to be crewing one of the other garage's buses. Behind the Bristol VR is No. 2674, (A674 UOE), an MCW 'Metrobus' DR102/27 MkII, belonging to the next generation of buses to be used on the No. 529 route. The buses would leave this terminus and turn hard right into Station Street.

(D. R. Harvey Collection)

Many years after the trolleybuses had been withdrawn the No. 529 route had its terminus altered again when it moved into St Paul's Bus Station after the Park Street pedestrianisation scheme was completed in 1996. Travelling down St Paul's Street alongside the bus station is the first of the fifteen WMT Alexander 'Ultra'-bodied Volvo B10Ls dating from 1997. No. 1501, (P501 KOX), is working on the No. 29 service on 21 July 1997. These new route-branded Volvo B10L buses operating on the No. 529 route were the first Compressed Natural Gas (CNG) powered buses in the United Kingdom. On the right in the soon to be replaced herring-bone stands of Walsall's 1930s bus station is a Mark I MCW 'Metrobus', No. 2135, (GOG 135W).

(D. R. Harvey)

Standing alongside the ABC Cinema in Green Lane at the new unloading point is Wolverhampton Corporation's 493, (FJW 493). This Park Royal-bodied Guy BT is unloading passengers in 1963 just before turning left into Townend Street. The ABC is showing 'Tales of Terror' based on three short stories by Edgar Allan Poe starring Vincent Price, Peter Lorre, and Basil Rathbone. In the distance is a Sunbeam F4A trolleybus operating on the No. 33 service to Cavendish Avenue.

(A. B. Cross)

Travelling towards Walsall town centre in Stafford Street at Proffitt Street is No. 897, (897 MDH). It is coming from Birchills garage and is on its way to Townend Street to take up duties on the 29 route. This was one of five 30ft long AEC 'Regent' V 2D2RAs with Willowbrook H41/31F bodies introduced in August and September 1961 along with five other AECs with Metro-Cammell bodies and five MCCW-bodied Daimler CVG6/30s. After the closure of the No. 29 trolleybus route in 1965, these fifteen high-capacity, forward-entrance buses were used on the Walsall and Wolverhampton joint service along with Wolverhampton's 30ft long Guy 'Arab' IVs and Vs. Unfortunately these Walsall vehicles seemed to be very camera-shy on the No. 29 route.

(D. F. Parker)

For nineteen of the thirty-four years during which the No. 29 service operated, the route used the Savoy Cinema, later to become the ABC Cinema, as an anticlockwise terminal loop. Waiting to load up in Townend Street in April 1952 is Sunbeam W4 326, (JDH 333), formerly numbered 231. This wartime trolleybus was fitted with a Brush fifty-six-seat body built to MoWT specifications, and it had entered service on 29 June 1945. Behind the trolleybus is Green Lane, long before it was wired up for the No. 33 route to Cavendish Avenue.

(D. F. Parker)

Walsall Corporation purchased eight Park Royal-bodied Sunbeam F4 trolleybuses from Ipswich Corporation between February and May 1962. There were twelve trolleybuses in the batch numbered 115 to 126, but Walsall only had 119-126 as the first four of the batch were retained by Ipswich until the closure of their trolleybus system on 23 August 1963. Taking its turn in the queue in Townend Street on 22 July 1963 is 351, (ADX 189), which had been numbered 119 in the Ipswich fleet. It has just turned from Green Lane where on the distant wall opposite the entrance to Townend Street is Hewitt's footwear advertisement. Hewitt's Boot Store was located in Stafford Street on the corner of Wisemore.

(D. R. Harvey Collection)

The abandonment of the joint inter-urban No. 29 trolleybus route took place on 31 October 1965. The replacement bus service retained the service number 29 and used the same loop around the ABC Cinema picking up passengers in Townend Street. No. 900, (900 MDH), the last of five AEC 'Regent' V 2D2RAs with Willowbrook H41/31F bodies, which entered service in September 1961, loads up before embarking on the 7 mile journey back to Wolverhampton. The trolleybus overhead is still in place as the loop behind the cinema was subsequently used by the No. 33 service. Travelling into the town centre is No. 869, (XDH 69), one of the 'Goldfish Bowls', a 30ft long Willowbrook-bodied Sunbeam F4As working on a No. 33 route from Cavendish Avenue before this loop was brought into use.

(R. F. Mack)

The first trolleybuses bought to full post-war standards were also the last trolleybuses ordered by Mr Somerfield. These 7ft 6in wide Sunbeam F4s had bodywork by Brush and their interiors were better appointed than the contemporary Walsall motorbuses whose Park Royal bodies were spartan in the extreme. Trolleybus No. 343, (NDH 960), which had entered service on 23 November 1951, is standing Townend Street opposite the corner of Shaw Street. The almost new No. 343 is still in its original dark and mid-blue livery.

(C. Carter)

No. 309, (BDY 816), is unloading in Wolverhampton Street on 19 May 1963. It is alongside the ABC Cinema and will turn left into Green Lane from Townend before turning left again into Townend Street where it would load up again for the journey back to Wolverhampton. Behind this former Hastings Tramways Weymann-bodied Sunbeam W4 is a Wolverhampton trolleybus turning out of Townend Street into Wolverhampton Street.

(W. Ryan)

No. 334, (NDH 951), was the first of the Brush-bodied Sunbeam F4s. It was delivered in December 1950, some ten months before the next vehicles in the class entered service, as this trolleybus was the former Commercial Motor Show Exhibit of 1950. On 25 July 1952, No. 334 comes out of Townend Street at the rear of the Savoy Cinema just before its driver begins the left turn into Wolverhampton Street. The trolleybus is in the two-tone blue livery which would be replaced in the next few years by the recently appointed general manager. Behind the trolleybus is the local warehouse of W. H. Smith, the bookseller and stationer. The frequency of the joint service between Walsall and Wolverhampton varied between every six minutes in the peak periods and every eleven minutes at all other times, with the first service leaving Walsall at 5.55am and the last departure leaving both termini at 11pm.

(C. W. Routh)

Turning into Wolverhampton Street from Townend Street on an extremely unpleasant day is trolleybus 345, (ADX 194). This Park Royal-bodied Sunbeam F4 had formerly been Ipswich Corporation's No. 124 and had entered service in Walsall on 18 April 1962. It is 3.10pm and the interior lights of the trolleybus have already been switched on. The parked car which No. 345's driver has studiously avoided is a Ford Consul II 204E. Behind the trolleybus is the imposing ABC Cinema, while in the distance are the shops at the top of Park Street. The cinema, which had been designed by R. G. Madeley in 1936, was demolished in 1995 and replaced by a new Woolworth's store which succumbed in December 2008. On the left, on the corner of Townend Street, is the Leather Shop.

(J. C. Brown)

Travelling along Wolverhampton Street towards the setting down terminus of the 29 service is Wolverhampton 498, (FJW 498), a Guy BT with a Park Royal H28/26R body. The trolleybus is passing the premises of the Leather Shop. This shop was located on the corner of Townend Street and seems to have an extensive selection of trunks and suitcases in the window. Behind the trolleybus is the impressive four-storey Edwardian premises of John More, fancy leather goods manufacturers.

(C. Carter)

Speeding along Wolverhampton Street in May 1962, with Blue Lane West leading to Green Lane on the left, is the freshly repainted Guy BT 496, (FJW 496). This Park Royal-bodied trolleybus belonging to Wolverhampton Corporation is working on the 29 route. Behind the trolleybus, being passed by a Vauxhall Velox PASX, is the mid-Victorian Engine Inn. Beyond the pub is a Duple Vista-bodied Bedford SB coach which is approaching the ABC Cinema.

(D. Wilson)

31

Having crossed the Pleck Road junction, the trolleybuses travelling inbound to Walsall immediately crossed the Walsall Canal at Canal Street. The trolleybus is No. 309, (BDY 816), a Weymann-bodied Sunbeam W4, formerly operated by Hastings Tramways as their No. 41 and sold to Walsall in June 1959 by Maidstone & District, who had taken over the Hastings system in October 1957. The trolleybus is in Wolverhampton Street and is passing the Butler's Brewery-owned Elephant & Castle public house. The impressive building on the right is the Albion Flour Mill, built in 1848 and still being used as a flour mill until the mid-1970s. After being derelict for many years, this fine example of mid-nineteenth-century industrial architecture is being transformed into luxury apartments.

(D. Wilson)

Climbing up Wolverhampton Road from Willenhall is another of the powerful 95hp Sunbeam F4 trolleybuses acquired from Ipswich Corporation in 1962. Having 95hp motors, like the former Hastings Tramways trolleybuses acquired in 1959, the Ipswich trolleybuses were quickly put into service on the Wolverhampton joint service where their performance was very impressive. Trolleybus 353, (ADX 191), is overtaking a parked Morris 1100 near Pargeter Street and, although the road is lined with Victorian terraced housing, the trolleybus is by now almost at the edge of the town centre.

(J. C. Brown)

Above: At the bottom of the long hill in Wolverhampton Road in Bentley is No. 352, (ADX 190). The trolleybus has just passed the junction with Primley Avenue, which is where the house on the right is located, and is about to pass beneath the electricity feeder cables, necessitating coasting across that position on the overhead. Opposite the trolleybus and to the right of the two cyclists who are somewhat hogging the Walsall-bound carriageway is the Bridge Inn. The destination boxes on these former Ipswich Corporation Sunbeam F4 trolleybuses could accommodate the word 'Walsall' in the aperture, but the word 'Wolverhampton' was too long. So the ingenious diagonal method of displaying this destination was made.

(J. C. Brown)

Opposite, top: Climbing up the hill in Wolverhampton Road, Bentley, from Anson Bridge is No. 345, (ADX 194). The Park Royal bodywork on this former Ipswich Sunbeam F4s batch was considerably different, particularly at the front of the upper saloon, to the Wolverhampton Corporation examples built on similar Sunbeam F4 chassis or their unique batch of Guy BTs. No. 345 is approaching the huge civil engineering work being undertaken at the time as exemplified by the mud on the road in the foreground. This was part of the construction of the M6 motorway and specifically the Junction 10 complex. It had only been a few years earlier on 2 September 1963 that Walsall's last trolleybus extension along Bloxwich Lane had been opened, confusingly numbered 33, with the alternative of making another loop along Cavendish Road. A second proposal was to extend the service along Bloxwich Lane to join up with the 29 inter-urban service at Bentley, which could have provided a direct trolleybus link between Willenhall and Bloxwich. With the imminent construction of the M6 cutting through Bentley, this, of course, never got beyond the planning stage.

(J. C. Brown)

Below: An agreement had been reached between Walsall and Wolverhampton Corporation that the joint trolleybus service would be retained until 1967 irrespective of the rest of Wolverhampton's abandonment programme. Unfortunately, the line of the new M6 motorway cut across the line of the 29 trolleybus route at Anson Bridge, Bentley, and as if to put a further nail in the operating coffin, Bentley was also chosen to be the site of the complex road layout of the motorway's Junction 10! The large warning sign on the left in Wolverhampton Road really sounds the death knell for the trolleybus route. Despite soldiering on for many months with construction traffic and preliminary road deviations the 29 route succumbed to the inevitable and was closed on 31 October 1965. Walsall's 351, (ADX 189), a former Ipswich Corporation Park Royal-bodied Sunbeam F4, has just negotiated a set of temporary traffic lights as it travels towards Willenhall, while passing in the opposite direction is Wolverhampton's 638, (FJW 638), a Guy BT with a Park Royal H28/26R body.

(D. R. Harvey Collection)

Bentley Cemetery in Wolverhampton Road West was opened in 1898 for Willenhall UDC. Passing the iron railings of the cemetery is No. 335, (NDH 952), one of the 1951 Brush-bodied Sunbeam F4s on its way towards Wolverhampton. The all-over blue livery did nothing to improve their image. Behind the trolleybus is a row of 1930s housing with its own service road. The trolleybus is passing a Vauxhall Victor F Series II car dating from about 1960, which although only about five years old is already exhibiting signs of body rot – the tin worm was a terrible problem for Vauxhall cars of this vintage.

(J. C. Brown)

Walsall's 346, (ADX 195) crosses the brick-built bridge over the Bentley Branch Canal. The canal had been opened in 1843 as part of the Birmingham Canal navigations network and passes alongside the cemetery. This canal was part of the Birmingham Canal Navigation network and was built to provide a 3-mile shortcut between Wolverhampton and the main Walsall Branch of the BCN. It was officially abandoned in 1961 about four years before 346 was photographed descending from Bentley. This Park Royal-bodied Sunbeam F4 is travelling down the hill towards the distant junction with Clarkes Lane in Wolverhampton Road West. On the skyline are the fifteen-storey flats in Bentley.

(J. C. Brown)

On a rainy day in 1965, No. 346, (ADX 195), a former Ipswich Corporation Sunbeam F4, travels towards Wolverhampton, despite the incorrect destination box display. The electric overhead feeder cables are on the left hand side of the road, revealing that the trolleybus is still on the Walsall side of the electric supply beyond the cemetery in Wolverhampton Road West as it approaches Willenhall. Travelling in the opposite direction is a 1958 Vauxhall Victor F saloon, while parked in the service road in front of the 1930s houses is a Vauxhall Velox and a Morris Minor 1000 two-door saloon.

(J. C. Brown)

Speeding out of the centre of Willenhall in Walsall Street is, yet again, Walsall trolleybus No. 346, (ADX 195). The vehicle is travelling towards Walsall and has negotiated the tight section of road alongside St Giles' parish church, where the 'road-narrows' sign is located. The trolleybus is about to pass King Street on the right, while behind it is a late eighteenth-century house at the entrance of Church Street with Doctor's Piece being hidden behind the trolleybus. On the right beyond the post office and the child on its fairy cycle are the tall early nineteenth-century premises of T.B. Wolverson. They were originally established in 1924 and are still a leading independent supplier of industrial X-Ray and innovative imaging equipment. Behind the Wolverson premises is the Prince of Wales public house.

(J. C. Brown)

Civic and transport dignitaries pose in front of one of the Sunbeam MS2s from the 160-164 batch of Short-bodied trolleybuses, all of which entered service on 1 October 1933. The trolleybus is parked alongside the churchyard of St Giles' in Willenhall and is giving a demonstration of the new trolleybus to these invited guests.

(D. R. Harvey Collection)

Standing in the trolleybus lay-by in Walsall Street is Walsall's 352, (ADX 190). This Sunbeam F4 had a Park Royal H30/26R body and was acquired from Ipswich Corporation where it was numbered 120 in that municipality's fleet. The lay-by in front of the splendid parish church of St Giles was used by all trolleybuses going towards Wolverhampton. St Giles' church was designed by W. D. Griffin, an architect based in Wolverhampton, and was consecrated in 1867. On the distant bend is the Prince of Wales public house.

(D. A. Jones)

Standing in Walsall Street in the centre of Willenhall, at the halfway point on the 29 route between Wolverhampton and Walsall, is a well-laden 322, (JDH 29); it had been re-numbered from 225 in October 1950. This Sunbeam W4 had a Park Royal body and a Metro-Vickers 207A3 85hp motor. This trolleybus was one of the earliest of the wartime trolleybuses to be withdrawn, this occurring in December 1959. No. 322 is waiting beyond the Royal George public house and the wonderful nineteenth-century Market Place. The trolleybus, apparently still in its original two-tone blue livery, is about to set off towards Walsall, though a destination number box aperture was never fitted to any of Walsall's wartime vehicles.

(C. Carter)

Taking part on a trial run before the opening of the joint trolleybus operation with Wolverhampton Corporation is No. 151, (DH 8313). This AEC 663T six-wheeler was fitted with an English Electric body with full-depth vertically-sliding upper saloon windows. It was virtually the same as the three prototype 663Ts, whose bodies were quickly replaced after about two years of being employed as AEC demonstrators. The bus is standing outside the Royal George public house in Walsall Street, Willenhall, with members of the Transport Committee and Mr William Vane Morland, the general manager, standing to the left of the cab door. The 29 service would be his only venture into trolleybus operation as he took over control at Leeds City Transport on Friday 1 April 1932 well before the second trolleybus service to Bloxwich was opened. Mr Morland even took the Walsall turquoise blue livery with him to Yorkshire.

(D. R. Harvey Collection)

Parked outside the Royal George public house in Walsall Street, Willenhall in about 1935 is the last of the Short-bodied Sunbeam MS2s. No. 164, (ADH10), is on its way to Walsall but the crew had a long enough break at this half way point of the 29 route to pose in the summer sunshine for the photographer. By this time the staircase window has been plated over on the grounds of decency. The trolleybus is carrying an advertisement for the Rosum Cinema in Leamore on the Bloxwich trolleybus route.

(D. R. Harvey Collection)

Coming from Walsall into Willenhall with Walsall Street behind it in about 1964 is No. 341, (NDH 958). This was one of the ten Walsall Corporation trolleybuses entering service on 1 November 1951. It was a Brush H30/26R-bodied Sunbeam F4 fitted with powerful BTH 95hp motors. The trolleybus is now painted in the all-over pale blue livery. It now draws its electricity from Wolverhampton's power supply, which started at the splitting point at the double set of wires above the Belisha Beacon on the right. Behind the trolleybus is the Royal George public house, dating from 1847, which, despite the sign, had been owned by Mitchells & Butlers since 1959. Following the trolleybus out of Walsall Street is a Morris-Commercial LC4 truck.

(W. J. Haynes)

The driver of Wolverhampton Corporation 477, (FJW 477), hauls the Park Royal-bodied Sunbeam F4 around the traffic island in the middle of Willenhall. With the Atkinson-signed Royal George public house in the background, the trolleybus, working on the No. 5 route, has come from New Road on the left and will undertake this 180° turn across the bottom of Bilston Street which is where the interurban 25 trolleybus route terminated.

Under the terms of the M & B take over, all Atkinson's pubs had to retain their original pub signs for the next ten years – which is why the Royal George appears to retain its Atkinson ownership.

(D. R. Harvey Collection)

One of the former Ipswich Corporation trolleybuses, 345, (ADX 194), turns back at Willenhall Market Place into Walsall Street as it returns to Walsall. The trolleybus has turned in front of the turreted Midland Bank on the corner of New Street and the Market Place. This impressive building had been built in the last decade of Queen Victoria's reign for the Metropolitan Bank. The manoeuvre was undertaken by all the original four Walsall trolleybuses between the opening of the first trolley bus route on 22 July 1931 and the introduction of the joint working of double-deck trolleybuses between Walsall and Wolverhampton on 6 November 1931. Once the through service was established Wolverhampton provided the electricity around the traffic island at a charge of a levy of 2s 6d per 100 workings.

(J. G. Simpson)

The entrance to the now-pedestrianised Market Place in Willenhall enabled a bus lay-by to be created between the impressively turreted Victorian premises of the HSBC Bank and the Royal George public house. Travel West Midland 4683 (BX54 XTA), a Volvo B7TL with a Wright 71-seat body fitted with coach seats, loads up with passengers when working on the No. 529 service on 4 May 2009. To the left, New Road disappears in a westerly direction looking towards the Willenhall Lock Museum and Wolverhampton.

(D. R. Harvey)

The Willenhall terminus of the No. 25 service from Fighting Cocks and Bilston was at the bottom of Rose Hill in Bilston Street. Having arrived in Willenhall on the 25 route, the trolleybuses turned around the traffic island, crossing the Walsall to Wolverhampton service where New Road and Walsall Street met before returning to Bilston Street. Because of the overhead layout it was possible for a trolleybus to change routes but this would have necessitated repolling the trolley booms and this manoeuvre was rarely undertaken. Behind the trolleybus is the Railway Tavern public house. Wolverhampton 478, (FJW 478), a 1948-vintage Sunbeam F4 with a Park Royal body, waits at the terminus before starting off to Fighting Cocks on the No. 25 route. Behind it, crossing from Walsall Street into New Road on the 29 route towards Wolverhampton, is Walsall's 308, (BDY 814), a 1947-built Sunbeam W4 with a Weymann H30/26R body that had formerly been Hastings Tramways 39.

(C. W. Routh)

Once beyond Willenhall, the jointly operated trolleybus ran under the wires of Wolverhampton Corporation. On the occasion of a trolleybus tour in 1961, Walsall's 30ft long Willowbrook-bodied Sunbeam F4A 870, (XDH 70), was used as the tour trolleybus and the opportunity was taken to drive a Walsall trolleybus over routes it would otherwise never reach. Walsall Corporation 870, (XDH 70), is in New Road standing behind an unidentified Wolverhampton trolleybus working on the 29 route. The pair of trolleybuses is facing the Market Place junction. Walsall's 870 was one of the seven Sunbeam F4As with a Willowbrook H36/34RD body delivered during 1956. These 30ft-long trolleybuses were not used on the jointly operated 29 route because their seating capacity was 23% greater than the usual trolleybuses operated by Wolverhampton.

(D. Williams)

46

Leaving Willenhall by way of New Road is Wolverhampton's 404, (DJW 904). This Sunbeam W4 chassis dated from 1944 and was re-bodied by Park Royal in 1952 in this very dated style. The trolleybus is leaving the centre of Willenhall on the 29 route and is passing on the left the junction with Wolverhampton Street. New Road was so named when it opened in 1818 to improve access between Willenhall and Wolverhampton. The town of Willenhall was famous for its lock manufacturers such as Legge, Squire and Yale, and in New Road is the marvellous Willenhall Lock Museum.

(J. C. Brown)

Portobello was a small village that grew-up along the Wolverhampton to Walsall Road on the western edge of Willenhall. This suburb of Willenhall almost disappeared in the 1970s when the road became a dual carriageway. Crossing the former L&NWR Grand Junction railway line at Portobello Bridge is the former Ipswich Corporation trolleybus 126. By now numbered 347 in the Walsall fleet, ADX 196, a Sunbeam F4 with a Park Royal H30/26R body, is passing the Bridge public house as it travels on the 29 route towards Wolverhampton. Behind the trolleybus is the Westley Court block of flats, one of three blocks built by the erstwhile Willenhall UDC. This 95hp-motored trolleybus entered service in the Suffolk town in July 1950. It entered service with Walsall in February 1962 and would survive in service until February 1970.

(J. C. Brown)

The trolleybus wiring has not long been dismantled but the traction poles are still in place in Willenhall Road, Moseley in 1967. Travelling along Willenhall Road towards Wolverhampton is the unique No. 22, (YDA 22). It is passing the Rydal Green flats near Deans Road and is working on the shortworking of the 5 route from Willenhall. This Guy 'Arab' IV was originally fitted with full-front, Metro-Cammell, forward-entrance, seventy-two-seat bodywork. However, it was converted in 1966 from its original full-front specification to a half-cab, while retaining its original radiator grill, as an experiment in an attempt to get better access to the Gardner 6LW engine. The bus is being overtaken by a well-laden Austin Farina A40.

(R. Marshall)

Passing the Merry Boys public house on the corner of Deans Road is former Ipswich trolleybus No. 354 (ADX 192). The traction poles along Willenhall Road from Stow Hill Lane/Deans Road towards Willenhall originally belonged to the Wolverhampton District Electric Tramways, and these could be identified by the decorative finials on the top of the poles. Tram services towards Wolverhampton were operated by Wolverhampton Corporation on the Lorain surface contact stud method. The whole of this section of Willenhall Road was redeveloped in the 1950s and the pub and the block of three-storey flats, beyond the approaching Total Oil-owned Atkinson articulated tanker lorry, belong to this period and survive today. Half hidden by the 1961 Vauxhall Victor FB turning right into Deans Road is a Commer Superpoise ¾ton van dating from 1957.

(R. F. Mack)

Once onto the long, straight section of Willenhall Road the trolleybuses were able to 'stretch their legs' and the need for some performance led to Walsall employing 95hp-motored trolleybuses. This matched the power of the 8ft wide post-war Wolverhampton trolleybuses. As Wolverhampton's trolleybuses had a seating capacity of only between fifty-four and sixty seats, Walsall was compelled to use trolleybuses of a similar size, which is why the 1955-6 Sunbeam F4As were not used on the 29 service. The need for more trolleybuses with 95hp motors was one of the reasons why Walsall began to venture into the second-hand market. Sunbeam W4 308, (BDY 814), the former Hastings Tramways 39, had a Weymann H30/26R body and is speeding towards Wolverhampton soon after it entered service on 19 August 1959. It is passing the 1950s three-storey flats in Willenhall Road with Tyburn Road being hidden on the other side of the road by the trolleybus.

(R. F. Mack)

The Victorian terraced houses in Willenhall Road were still looking well cared for in about 1964. Passing Brooklands Parade is another of the former Ipswich Corporation trolleybuses. No. 353, (ADX 191), is travelling towards Willenhall from Wolverhampton on the 29 service with what appears to be an almost complete complement of passengers. The unusual car parked in front of the long-since-demolished Mayfield Flats in Willenhall Road is an NSU Prinz 583cc two-cylinder saloon owned by the photographer.

(J. C. Brown)

The 29 route was ideally suited to the interurban service between Walsall and Wolverhampton as it involved sections of flat, straight sections of road with long stretches between stages. No. 344, (ADX 193), an ex-Ipswich Sunbeam F4, travels towards Wolverhampton and is passing St Giles Crescent near Coventry Street on the left. Behind the trolleybus is the Wesleyan Reform Bethel Chapel. Lansdowne Terrace on the right, with its reconditioned mortar, forms part of the Victorian terrace in Willenhall Road.

(J. C. Brown)

In the distance a Ford Consul EOTTA 1508 cc four-door saloon comes out of Cross Street on the left. The trolleybus has come out of Lower Horseley Fields, which is hidden by the tipper lorry, while the road forking to the left is Lower Walsall Street. Opposite the car is Eastfield School, which was a Board School built as a result of the 1870 Education Act. Passing the school is Walsall trolleybus No. 347, (ADX 196). This Park Royal-bodied Sunbeam F4 is travelling out of Wolverhampton town centre near Colliery Road, which is hidden behind the trolleybus. Between the school and the distant Deans Road, a distance of nearly one mile, Willenhall Road was lined with late nineteenth-century, tunnel-backed houses only as far as Coventry Street whereupon this area of Stow Heath was littered with old coal mine shafts, slag heaps and several brickworks.

(J. C. Brown)

Travelling along Lower Horseley Fields in about 1964 is Wolverhampton trolleybus No. 440, (EJW 440), working on the 29 route towards its hometown. The Sunbeam W4 chassis entered service in April 1947 carrying a Park Royal body and was re-bodied with this attractive Roe H32/28R body in February 1961. This vehicle had been at Park Lane until all trolleybus operations from the garage were withdrawn in 1964. No. 440 would only have a short period working from Cleveland Road, as it was an early withdrawal having been involved in an accident in January 1965. It is passing James Summerhill's early post-war office block. The company was established in 1877 and specialised in the manufacturing of aluminium, alloy and steel corrugated sheet under the name of Beaver Star Brand.

(A. B. Cross)

Looking towards Lower Horseley Fields, with Summerhill's office block just visible, is trolleybus 353, (ADX 191). This Park Royal-bodied Sunbeam F4 is travelling into Wolverhampton having passed beneath the Horseley Fields railway bridge. These former Ipswich Corporation trolleybuses were used almost exclusively on the 29 service from when they were purchased in 1962 until the route was closed at the end of October 1965. When Wolverhampton Corporation introduced trolleybuses on the Willenhall service they had to use single-deck vehicles because of the lack of height between the railway bridge and the road; after much wrangling with the LMS Railway, the roadway was lowered to enable double-deck vehicles to pass unhindered beneath the railway bridge. The service to Willenhall reopened just nine days before the joint operation with Walsall was due to begin. On the left are the wharf buildings of H. Harvey, while on the right is Ever Ready's Canal Works, which used to belong to AJS who made cars and radios.

(A. B. Cross)

With its interior lights blazing No. 303, (BDY 806), one of the eight Weymann-bodied Sunbeam W4s purchased in 1959 from Maidstone & District, is about to emerge from the gloom of the Horseley Fields Bridge. By this time the saloon windows of these trolleybuses had all been rebuilt and fitted in white rubber mountings which did little to enhance the appearance of the vehicles. The railings on the raised pavement to the right of the trolleybus reveal the amount by which the Horseley Fields railway bridge was lowered in 1931. The bridge in the background with the Bull's Head Garage alongside it is over the BCN's James Brindley-designed Wolverhampton Level Canal, finished in 1772.

(A. B. Cross)

Just entering Lower Horseley Fields and passing over the BCN canal bridge is another of the Wolverhampton fleet of early post-war Sunbeam W4 trolleybuses which had been re-bodied by Charles Roe in January 1962. In this case, 436, (EJW 436), only lasted barely four years with its new body before it was prematurely withdrawn. The terrace building on the right, alongside the Thames 15cwt van, dates from about the mid-1850s, which is contemporary to the adjacent but well hidden canal cut.

(R. F. Mack)

The large Victorian factory building owned by Edward Vaughan Stampings Ltd, who produced quality drop forgings, dominated the north side of Horseley Fields. The three-storey building with its porthole windows usually cast a gloom over the road but on this sunny day it just looked an impressive piece of industrial architecture. Trolleybus 345, (ADX 194), an ex-Ipswich vehicle, seems to have its diagonal Wolverhampton destination blind ripped. It travels towards the left turn into Union Street and passes an Austin A40 Devon four-door saloon – registered in Staffordshire in 1949 – parked on the other side of the road.

(R. F. Mack)

The ladies look a little apprehensive as the trolleybus turns left only about five feet away from where they are standing. Wolverhampton's 635, (FJW 635), a 1950 Guy BT with a fifty-four-seat, 8ft wide Park Royal body, is entering Union Street from Horseley Fields on its way to the St James' Square terminus of the 29 route. The building on the left was owned by a branch of Walsall's Electrical Conduits Ltd, an electrical wholesaler supplying cabling, conduits and jointing to electrical contractors in the building trade. Behind the trolleybus in Horseley Fields is C. E. Teecey, a well-respected family butcher who had an early refrigerated-display meat cabinet in his window.

(R. F. Mack)

This bus entered service for Walsall Corporation, but after the closure of the Walsall to Wolverhampton trolleybus operation it was No. 93, (RDH 93F). This Daimler 'Fleetline' CRG6LX had a Northern Counties H41/29D body and had entered service in March 1968. During the last year of municipal operation the Walsall share of the joint service was increasingly operated by these strange-looking dual-door short-length rear-engined buses. The tall, early nineteenth-century building on the corner of the distant Little Park Street and Union Street had latterly been used by the Wolverhampton Boxing Club as their headquarters.

(J. C. Walker)

Still painted in its original two-tone blue livery is Walsall's 338, (NDH 955). The trolleybus is correctly parked in St James Square alongside the rear of the Walsall Street Institute. As well as having some impressive Georgian buildings, St James' Square was the location of Wolverhampton's most important Synagogue. It has arrived on the No. 29 route from its hometown. This Sunbeam F4 had a powerful BTH 95hp motor and a Brush fifty-six seat body. It had entered service in November 1951 just after the new St James' Square terminus of the 29 route was introduced. No. 338 would survive until the closure of the system by WMPTE in October 1970. The trolleybuses began using St James' Square after 15 October 1951 when the wiring across the Piper's Row junction was removed because of the increase in traffic congestion at the top of Horseley Fields.

(M. Rooum)

Pulling away from the utilitarian bus shelters in St James' Square is 305, (BDY 811), one of the eight former Hastings Tramways Sunbeam W4s with Weymann H30/26R bodies. By this time, in about 1963, all the twelve former Hastings Tramways trolleybuses sold to Bradford Corporation had been withdrawn. Most of the buildings in St James' Square were suffering from planning blight and some demolition had already taken place (some of which is visible behind the Duple-bodied Bedford SB coach).

(V. Nutton)

St James' Square, built in around 1750, was once a large elegant Georgian Square. It's not hard to imagine how good St James' Square must have looked in its heyday. In the 1950s and 1960s it was busy bustling area as it was the main bus terminus for the local motorbus and trolleybus routes to Willenhall, Bentley and Walsall. Pulling away from the Walsall Street Institute bus shelters is another of the Brush-bodied Sunbeam F4s dating from 1951. No. 341, (NDH 958), travels out of the square in about 1955 on its way into Horseley Fields. The strange box structure below the nearside lower saloon windows held the trolley retrieval pole used to re-pole the trolleybus if it became de-wired.

(R. F. Mack)

Coming out of St James' Square, in about 1963, is one of the 1951 batch of trolleybuses bought new by Walsall Corporation. Even at this relatively late stage of its career, this trolleybus, No. 339 (NDH 956), although repainted in the all-over blue livery with a single thin yellow band between decks, still has a vestige of the original livery having managed to retain the three black livery bands around the bodywork. It is noticeable that the nearside windscreen had been rebuilt with rubber-mounted glass. Until the early 1960s, the shop on the corner of Horseley Fields and St James' Square had been Woodall's clothes and shoe shop but by 1964 it had become the premises of George Cheadle, a builder's merchant.

(D. R. Harvey Collection)

Having returned into Horseley Fields from St James Square the outbound trolleybuses almost immediately passed Bradshaw Street where the rather tatty advertisement for Mansion Polish has been posted on the brickwork. On the corner, hidden by the trolleybus, are the premises of K. D. Biddlestone who sold second-hand cookers, fires and household supplies. Next door is the Mitchells & Butler-owned Star Vaults pub and in the doorway on the right is a bottle of sterilized milk, a type of milk extensively used throughout the West Midlands in the days before refrigeration was common. Walsall 345, (ADX 194), a former Ipswich Corporation Park Royal-bodied 95hp Sunbeam F4, begins its long journey to Willenhall and Walsall.

(R. F. Mack)

In about 1935, No. 169, (ADH 15), a two-year old Sunbeam MS2 with a Weymann H32/289R body, which was later renumbered 315 in 1950, stands in Horseley Fields, Wolverhampton outside the Banks'-owned New Inns public house. It is working on the 29 service back to Walsall and is standing at the original terminus just beyond the junction with Old Mill Street. In their original light blue livery with cream bands and gold-lining out, these six-wheelers did look extremely smart and the advertisement for the locally brewery 'Highgate Mild Ales' enhances the whole effect.

(W. J. Haynes)

Standing at the rudimentary terminus shelters of the 29 route outside the New Inns public house, rebuilt in 1935 in Horseley Fields, is No. 326, (JDH 333). This trolleybus had formerly been No. 230 until it was renumbered in October 1950. Behind the trolleybus is the entrance to Old Mill Street and beyond that the side of the entrance building to the High Level Station. This trolleybus was a wartime Sunbeam W4 with a Brush H30/26R body dating from June 1945. For about five years these wartime trolleybuses were the mainstay of the Walsall share of the joint service. They were only reduced to more of a secondary role when the NDH-registered entered service after this original terminus was switched from Horseley Fields to St James' Square in October 1951.

(J. S. Webb)

The original Wolverhampton terminus of the jointly operated 29 service was in Horseley Fields. In order for the trolleybuses to turn round they had to enter a wiring loop at the junction of Piper's Row and Horseley Fields at the Five Ways end of Victoria Square. With London and North Western Hotel dating from 1890 in the background, Walsall's 237, (JDH 434), a wartime Sunbeam W4 with a Roe semi-utility H30/26R body dating from March 1946, pulls a hard right lock in front of the now-preserved entrance buildings to the former LNWR's High Level Railway Station as it returns into Horseley Fields. Built on the site of the Cock Inn, the L&NW Hotel became part of the Victoria Hotel next door and the complex survives today as the Britannia Hotel.

(J. Hughes)

The Wolverhampton bus station was refurbished in 2005 and has no less than twenty-one departure stands and five unloading stands on this one site. Loading up at the bus shelter, the brand new route-dedicated No. 529 waiting to go to Walsall is 4133, (Y726 TOH). This Dennis 'Trident' has an Alexander H47/28F body and entered service in April 2001. To the right of the bus is the preserved entrance building to the High Level Railway Station, while the 'Metrobus' parked in the background is roughly standing where the trolleybuses turned around at the top of Horseley Fields.

(A. E. Hall)

CHAPTER TWO

BLOXWICH ROUTE AT THE BRIDGE AND IN PARK STREET

The second Walsall trolleybus service to open was that to Bloxwich by way of Stafford Street, Bloxwich Road and High Street, Bloxwich. In Victorian times Bloxwich was a village separated from Walsall by coalmines and open cast excavations. The introduction of the South Staffordshire Tramways steam tram service on 4 December 1884 opened up passenger transport for the working people of Bloxwich and linked them not only to Walsall but also to Wednesbury and Darlaston by a regular public road transport service. By the first day of 1893, the whole 7½ mile route had been converted to electric operation, making it only the second system in the UK to be operated by overhead electric power, the first being at Roundhay, Leeds on 11 November 1891. The tram route to Bloxwich via Birchills and Leamore was the last Walsall Corporation route to close on Saturday 30 September 1933 and trolleybuses took over on the following day.

The new Bloxwich trolleybus service was numbered 30, and on arriving in the town centre where Stafford Street entered Townend it passed the turning circle for the 29 jointly operated service to Willenhall and Wolverhampton. It used Park Street to gain access to and also to leave the terminus at The Bridge, which was outside the famous George Hotel just in front of the statue of Sister Dora. In September 1950, with the opening of St Paul's Bus Station, the inward journey of the Bloxwich trolleybus service was diverted to travel down St Paul's Street. Here they turned right at St Paul's Church into The Bridge where they terminated outside the Burton's Tailor complex of shops which had replaced the George Hotel in 1935. This meant that the tight 180° loop in the Bridge was eliminated much to the pleasure of the trolleybus drivers working on the Bloxwich service who must have dreaded this manoeuvre. The trolleybuses then left the town centre as before by way of travelling up Park Street passing the railway station on the left before crossing Townend and re-entering Stafford Street and proceeding northwards to Leamore and Bloxwich.

A further change was made to the 30 route in 1955 when the loop through the town from The Bridge into Park Street was abandoned and the trolleybuses were rewired to undertake a new 180° turn outside St Paul's Church and back into St Paul's Bus Station; there they used the fourth loading platform, which was located in Park Street rather than in the bus station itself.

This chapter looks at the No. 30 route's original route into the town by way of Park Street and the terminus at The Bridge.

The trolleybus used to open the new No. 30 route to Bloxwich on 1 October 1933 was Sunbeam MS2 159, (ADH 5). This is also the first day in service for this Beadle H32/28R bodied six-wheeler. It is parked at The Bridge outside the original classically styled George Hotel, which had been built in 1781 as a coaching inn. Sister Dora looks benevolently down from her plinth and oversees the members of the Walsall Corporation Motor's Transport Committee, including the general manager, Mr M.J. Somerfield, who are posing for posterity on this auspicious day. Dorothy Pattison came to the town in 1865 as a nurse in the Sisterhood of the Good Samaritans, and in 1868 and 1869 she began a period of selfless nursing of patients who were victims of a smallpox epidemic. Her legendary nursing work led to the opening of Walsall's General Hospital in 1878, and her original white marble statue was unveiled on 11 October 1886.

(D. R. Harvey Collection)

In about 1948, Beadle-bodied Sunbeam MS2, 157, (ADH 3), stands at the bus shelters at The Bridge before departing on the No. 30 route to Bloxwich. Both The Bridge and the distant Lichfield Street, with its impressive late Victorian Renaissance-styled retail premises, were still the main route through the town from Lichfield towards Wednesbury. As a result, even for the ration book days of early post-war Britain, there is quite a lot of traffic including the wartime Bedford OXC articulated flatbed lorry with its military style bonnet. Dominating the scene is Walsall's own original 'four-faced' liar, showing the time as ten past three.

(D. R. Harvey Collection)

The original George Hotel had been demolished in 1933 and replaced two years later by the Art Deco-styled block of offices and shops which included a replacement George Hotel, Keys' radio and cycle shop and Montague Burton, the gentleman's 30/- tailor. In about 1950, 219, (HDH 214), stands at The Bridge bus shelters outside the arc of the 1935 Art Deco-styled George Hotel where the juxtaposition of the statue of Sister Dora, the idolised local heroine, and the subterranean public toilets always seemed strange. No. 219, a Sunbeam MS2 with a stylish Park Royal H32/28R body, entered service on 1 March 1940 making it the last double-deck MS2s to be delivered to a British trolleybus operator.

(R. Marshall)

Just pulling away from the bus shelters at The Bridge terminus is six-wheel trolleybus No. 166, (ADH 12). Still looking fairly new and painted in its original blue and white livery this was another 80hp Metro-Vickers (BT-H) motored Sunbeam MS2. No. 166 had a Weymann H32/28R body of composite construction and had entered service on the same day as the opening of the new Bloxwich service. Other than the prototype Sunbeam MS1 of May 1931 registered JW 526 and a batch of twelve Guy BTXs delivered in July 1933 to Derby Corporation these five were only the third set of composite bodies constructed on any sort of trolleybus chassis and all were notably six-wheelers. On the extreme right at the junction of St Paul's Street and The Bridge are the late nineteenth-century cupola-topped premises of the Midland Bank. 166 was the last of the 1933 trolleybuses to remain in service, somehow lingering on until the end of September 1956.

(D. R. Harvey Collection)

The first of the trolleybuses bought for the opening of the 33 route to Bloxwich was 155. Registered ADH 1, 'a registration to die for', this Sunbeam MS2 was bodied by Beadle with an H32/28R body and entered service in August 1933 when it was used for driver training. The Beadle-bodied MS2s could easily be distinguished from both the Short and the Weymann-bodied examples by the very short cab side front windows. On 23 August 1950, 155 is already loaded up to the gunwales with its sixty seated as well as standing passengers. There is still a long queue snaking around the Sister Dora statue to be accommodated by the second trolleybus, which is also one of the Beadle-bodied 155-159 batch. Behind the trolleybus and next to Lloyds Bank is Pattison's café whose cakes and pastries were delicious.

(Walsall Observer)

The rear of the fifteen trolleybuses which were bought for the opening of the Bloxwich service in 1933 looked considerably more modern than the front profile. No. 162, (ADX 8), a Short-bodied Sunbeam MS2, is in pristine condition in its attractive gold lined-out light blue and cream livery. The trolleybus is carrying an advertisement for Atkinson Ales. No. 162 is at the terminus at The Bridge alongside the statue of Sister Dora in the days before loading shelters were provided and is parked behind one of the Corporation's Dennis 'Lances'.

(D. R. Harvey Collection)

Looking from Pattison's café across The Bridge to the terminus of the 30 route to Bloxwich, trolleybus No. 163, (ADH 9), stands at the loading shelters. This Short Brothers-bodied Sunbeam MS2 is not doing much business on 23 August 1950, but is showing off the early post-war light and dark blue livery. Behind the trolleybus are the various Victorian premises including Grey's double-windowed premises and Burton's tailor shop in Digbeth.

(D. R. Harvey Collection)

Still with its sidelights covered and with wartime white blackout markings, No. 165, (ADH 11), turns around in the widest area of The Bridge at the bottom of St Paul's Street. This Weymann-bodied Sunbeam MS2 six-wheeler, painted in the immediate pre-war, semi-streamlined livery, is working on the 30 route to Bloxwich and shows clearly that this manoeuvre was undertaken without passengers being on board.

(D. R. Harvey Collection)

Although 343, (NDH 960), is displaying the wrong route number, photographs of trolleybuses running from the unloading point outside St Paul's Church along St Paul's Street towards The Bridge are extremely rare as it only happened between 1950 and 1955. In about 1952, when this Brush-bodied Sunbeam F4 was still quite new, the pristine No. 343 travels into the afternoon sunshine as it moves towards the shelters outside the George Hotel. Hidden by the trolleybus is Darwell Street to the right of the church.

(M. J. C. Dare)

Beadle-bodied Sunbeam MS2 159, (ADH 5), turns around at The Bridge in 1950. It is only a few days before this manoeuvre would be abandoned when the inbound Bloxwich trolleybuses were diverted to travel into The Bridge by way of St Paul's Street, which is the road in the background hidden by No. 159. Just visible between the rear of the trolleybus and Henry's shop can be seen a Corporation bus in St Paul's Bus Station. On the right and partly hidden by the trees is the Midland Bank dating from the late nineteenth century.

(J. S. Webb)

Turning on the hard right 180° lock that will bring it round to the loading shelters at The Bridge is 188, (EDH 864). On the right, Henry's 1930s department store stands on an important location on the corner of St Paul's Street. The trolleybus might be going on the shortworking to Leamore at the turning circle just to the north of the Rosum Cinema in Bloxwich Road, but should be displaying the route No. 34 rather than No. 28. Perhaps the conductor, who appears to be 'walking the trolleybus' around the loop at the junction with St Paul's Street, might have time to set the correct route number in the destination box. No. 188 was one of a pair of Sunbeam MS2 with a Park Royal H32/28R body and was first licensed on 28 February 1938.

(A. D. Packer)

An advertisement for Frank Mason advertising agency used Walsall's 157, (ADH 3), to illustrate the advantages of publicity and promotion of a product using the between decks panels of a bus. In this case it was for Parkinson's sugar coated pills. Parkinson's were a well-respected company based in Burnley who produced these tablets which eased back and kidney pains. In its original condition with the staircase exposed through a window at the offside rear of the trolleybus body, this Sunbeam MS2, with a Beadle-built body, waits outside Shipley's store, later to be owned by Henrys at The Bridge. The trolleybus is facing St Paul's Street and is about to turn round to pick up passengers outside the George Hotel.

(D. R. Harvey Collection)

In about 1947, trolleybus 217, (HDH 212), stands at The Bridge's unloading point facing the bottom of St Paul's Street. The trolleybus is a six-wheeled Sunbeam MS2 with a sixty-seat Park Royal body and on entering service on 1 February 1940 thereby becoming the last double-deck Sunbeam six-wheelers to be introduced in the United Kingdom before production ceased because of the wartime requirements. The trolleybus is still painted in the pre-war livery style of dark and light blue. The trolleybus is carrying an advertisement for 'Tizer the Appetizer', a red-coloured sweet and slightly fruity-tasting soft drink launched in 1924 by Fred Pickup of Manchester.

(D. R. Harvey Collection)

The first wartime trolleybuses were delivered in the immediate pre-war livery of dark and light blue where the lower deck dark blue panelling was applied in a streamlined style. Standing outside Lloyds Bank at The Bridge in October 1943 fitted with a full set of headlight masks and white edging paint is the two-month-old 226, (JDH 30). This was a Sunbeam W4 chassis with the original style of M. of S. type utility body built by Park Royal, which only had a single line destination box and therefore could only display the destination wording, in this case 'BLOXWICH'. These early wartime trolleybuses had just one pair of opening windows in each saloon and wooden slatted seating but did have a glazed upper saloon emergency exit. Nos. 225 and 226 were only the third batch of wartime trolleybus bodies to be constructed by Park Royal.

(J. S. Webb)

Trolleybus 160, (ADH 6), was the sixteenth Sunbeam MS2 to be built and was fitted with a Short Brothers H32/28R body. This trolleybus weighed 8 tons 8 cwt 3 qtrs and entered service on 1 October 1933 in time for the opening of the new Bloxwich route. It is about to turn into Park Street having left The Bridge terminus of the No. 30 service to Bloxwich in August 1950, just before the service was redirected. Behind the trolleybus is Lloyds Bank, with a veneer at street level made of Portland Stone, while on the right are the trees at the bottom of Park Street.

(C. Carter)

Wednesday 23 August 1950 was a miserable summer's day when trolleybus No. 165, (ADH 11), turns into The Bridge from Park Street. Dominating the corner is the imposing Lloyds Bank building, which opened for business during December 1904. This seventeen-year-old Weymann-bodied Sunbeam MS2 was working on the Bloxwich service just one week before the inbound wiring in Park Street was abandoned.

(J. S. Webb)

Looking from Park Street across The Bridge into Digbeth, also in August 1950, clearly shows the course taken by the Bloxwich trolleybuses in order to reach the terminus in front of the George Hotel. Just visible beyond the Lloyds Bank building on the left is a trolleybus standing at the terminus. Passing the bank in Park Street and about to turn left to the unloading point at The Bridge is trolleybus No. 159, (ADH 5), the last of the five 1933-vintage, Beadle-bodied Sunbeam MS2s. It survived until the last day of October 1951 when all ten of the Beadle and Short-bodied examples of six-wheelers were replaced by the ten NDH-registered, Brush-bodied Sunbeam F4s.

(J. S. Webb)

Standing outside Marsh & Baxter's pork butchers shop opposite the entrance to Walsall Railway Station in Park Street on the No. 30 route from Bloxwich is trolleybus No. 165, (ADH 11). This Weymann-bodied Sunbeam MS2, painted in the two-tone blue livery, is travelling into the town centre in June 1950. The elimination of painting black the rear bogie mudguards did little to enhance the appearance of some of these elderly trolleybuses giving them a very uncared for look. The trolleybus service between Bloxwich and Walsall had a frequency of between five and eight minutes during the week, though in the peak periods this was reduced to a trolleybus every four minutes. Next door is Chattin's café which seems to be attracting custom. In the distance is a bus standing in the wide space at the top of Park Street.

(J. S. Webb)

Despite looking a little tired, Weymann-bodied Sunbeam MS2 168, (ADH 14), was renumbered 314 in October 1950 when it was already seventeen years old. These five Weymann-bodied trolleybuses remained in service until at least February 1955, suggesting that the products of Addlestone were better than either the five Beadle or five Short Brothers Sunbeam MS2s bought at the same time. The trolleybus is standing in Park Street with the rather splendid canopy and booking hall at the entrance to Walsall railway station just behind it. To the right of the trolleybus are the remnants of the old Grand Theatre which stood on the corner of Park Street and Station Street. It was built in 1899 but was destroyed by fire in 1939 with the surviving ground floor becoming the Durham Ox public house. This does not appear to impress the Salvation Army officer who marches passed the pub's entrance without even a sideways look!

(J. H. Taylforth Collection)

On 3 June 1951, No. 314, (ADH 14), turns across Townend from Park Street before turning into Stafford Street. It is working on the 30 route to Bloxwich by way of Bloxwich Lane and Leamore. The Weymann-bodied Sunbeam MS2 had previously been numbered 168. The trolleybus is carrying a full load of passengers on this warm spring day when most of the half-drop saloon windows have been fully opened.

(V. C. Jones)

Travelling on an inbound 30 journey from Bloxwich is the first of the 1933-vintage, Weymann-bodied Sunbeam MS2. No. 165, (ADH 11), travels across Townend onto Park Street and is passing the three-storied late eighteenth-century buildings which contained the shop belonging to Marsh & Baxters, the Brierley Hill-based pork butchers. The trolleybus has come out of Stafford Street which is to the right of the semi-circular frontage of Richmond's kitchenware store where another outbound six-wheeler is travelling towards Bloxwich by way of Leamore. On the left is the wiring for the turning circle for the jointly worked 29 service to Wolverhampton.

(J. S. Webb)

Chapter Three

ST PAUL'S BUS STATION
AND ST PAUL'S STREET

St Paul's Bus Station was built in order to congregate the bus services going to the north, east and south of the town all in one place. The westerly routes had their terminus in Bradford Place and both termini were designed for buses rather than trolleybuses. The two pre-war routes to Wolverhampton and Bloxwich had their own separate termini in the town. Motorbuses began using the loading bays even before the new Transport Offices were occupied in July 1935, and prior to the official opening on 23 September 1937.

All buses entered the new Bus Station via Hatherton Road, which was a dual carriageway, with surplus buses parking along its length to St Paul's Street. Buses then departed onto The Bridge then via Lower Bridge Street for their destinations. By 1950 some properties in Lower Stafford Street, by the junction into Wisemore, were demolished to enable Bloxwich and Leamore trolley buses on the No. 30 route to divert via St Paul's Street, to gain access to The Bridge. Mr Edgley Cox's instituted the construction of a new set of trolleybus wires across the front of the Transport Offices from St Paul's Street. This immediately turned left and ran beside the rear of F.W. Woolworth's store before turning left again into the bottom of St Paul's Street opposite the church. This might have been a better arrangement than the 180° turn at Darwall Street except that it created a good deal of congestion; as a result the wiring was quickly abandoned in favour of the previously approved tight turn at the bottom of St Paul's Street. In 1955 the use of Park Street for trolleybus operation was abandoned when the Bloxwich trolleybuses started to use St Paul's Bus Station. They terminated just above St Paul's Church and then turned via a circle opposite St Paul's Church. They then used a surplus northerly-facing loading bay in St Paul's Street at the outer edge of the bus station. Sometime during the 1960s the bus station was also referred to as the Central Bus Station.

This section shows the bus station being used on all the trolleybus services from when they were first introduced in 1955 until the final trolleybus abandonment in West Midland PTE ownership in October 1970.

In September 1954, Brush-bodied Sunbeam F4 No. 340, (NDH 957), stands beneath the west window of the decorated Gothic-styled St Paul's Church that was completed in 1893 to the designs of J. L. Pearson, one of the leaders of the English Gothic Revival. The trolleybus is unloading at the utility shelters having arrived on the 30 route from Bloxwich. The overhead linesmen, using the ex-Birmingham AEC 'Mercury' Tower Wagon AOH 1 are doing some preparatory work before erecting the new trolleybus overhead wires. This would eliminate the need for the Bloxwich service to take the wiring on the top right into The Bridge. Soon, in 1955, the trolleybuses would do a 180° turn at the bollard and pull up to the top shelter on the St Paul's Street side of the bus shelter.

(J. Hughes Collection)

The first second-hand purchases made by Mr Edgley Cox were two-1946 vintage Karrier W4s which were numbered 14 and 15 in the Pontypridd UDC fleet. Purchased in December 1955 they were numbered 301 and 302 in the Walsall fleet. No. 301, (FTG 697), with a Roe semi-utility body and very similar to Walsall's own 234-237, has turned out of Stafford Street and is travelling along the short section of Wisemore before turning right into St Paul's Street and proceeding to the bus station.

(D. F. Parker)

As early as about 1960, rebuilding of the front upper deck windows on the NDH-registered Brush-bodied Sunbeam F4s was deemed necessary. No. 341, (NDH 958), with these windows already rebuilt, speeds past Walsall Technical College in St Paul's Street when working on an inbound 31 service from Abbey Square, Mossley. Behind the trolleybus is Wisemore and B. Deans wholesale warehouse, with its distinctive brick chimneys, which occupied the corner of Stafford Street and Wisemore. Following the trolleybus is a 1957 Walsall-registered, two-door Austin A35 and a large Daimler Majestic six-cylinder saloon.

(R. F. Mack)

Travelling out from St Paul's Bus Station is Sunbeam F4A 869, (XDH 69). It is travelling along the short length of Wisemore, which was used to link St Paul's Street with the junction with Park Street, Townend Street and Stafford Street. It would be the latter street into which No. 869 would turn in order to go on the anti-clockwise 15 service to Bloxwich. Behind the 30ft-long trolleybus are the Walsall Technical College buildings.

(D. R. Harvey Collection)

Leaving Walsall's station and passing over the long since disappeared decorative balustrade of the St Paul's Street bridge over the railway line is trolleybus No. 341, (NDH 958). The site of the bridge is now deeply buried beneath the 1990s Quasar Shopping Centre. With the exception of the all-over light blue livery, this 95hp Sunbeam F4 still has its Brush H30/26R body in its original condition. The trolleybus is working on the 30 route from Bloxwich and is being followed by a 1961-registered Morris FG Luton-bodied lorry whose radiator grill is missing.

(R. F. Mack)

The rebuilding of the wartime Park Royal body on Sunbeam W4 323, (JDH 30), was, again, largely restricted to the upper saloon front windows, although the opportunity to enlarge the one line destination box was not taken. No. 323, formerly No. 226, has just passed the Transport Offices opened in 1935 which were located at the north end of St Paul's bus station on 29 August 1959. At the time of writing, the building is boarded up and awaiting its fate.

(A. J. Douglas)

Standing beneath the Georgian cornice windows is six-wheeler 312, (ADH 12). The renumbering of the fifteen 1933 Sunbeam MS2s from 155 and 169 to 301-315 matched up the registrations to the new fleet numbers for the first time. Despite their age, the five Weymann-bodied trolleybuses were repainted in the all-over light blue livery. Looking positively sparkling, No. 312 has just unloaded having worked into the town on the No. 30 service from Bloxwich.

(R. Hannay)

Fresh from being exhibited at the 1950 Commercial Motor Show at Earl's Court, No. 334, (NDH 951), the first of the ten Brush-bodied Sunbeam F4s, stands in St Paul's Street at St Paul's Terrace. With its paintwork positively gleaming, the trolleybus has just arrived from Bloxwich on the 30 route and displays its sliding cab door. These were the first Walsall trolleybuses to have this feature. The early nineteenth-century building on the corner of St Paul's Street and St Paul's Terrace was occupied by the Birmingham-based Wesleyan & General Assurance Company. Parked in St Paul's Terrace is a Coventry-registered Morris 8 Series E dating from May 1939.

(D. R. Harvey Collection)

Standing across the entrance to St Paul's Terrace is the sole demonstrator borrowed by Walsall. The vehicle was on loan from Glasgow Corporation Transport from 19 February until 16 March 1953 and was Mr Edgley Cox's first attempt to persuade the good folk of Walsall that this was the trolleybus of the future. It must have been something of a shock to the passengers through Leamore and Bloxwich to see an orange, green and cream-liveried two-door single-decker plying along Bloxwich Road. Glasgow's TBS 2, (FYS 766), was a BUT RETB1 with a powerful English Electric 120hp motor and an East Lancashire B27D body. It had the capacity to carry another forty strap-hanging standee passengers and was not deemed a success by local passengers!

(D. R. Harvey Collection)

Above: On 26 March 1963, trolleybus 864, (TDH 914), stands outside St Paul's Church opposite the bus station having unloaded its passengers. The vehicle has arrived from the Eagle Hotel terminus of the 31 route in Cresswell Crescent, Mossley. The trolleybus is a 30ft-long Sunbeam F4A with a Willowbrook H36/34RD body. However, they were trail-blazing vehicles being the first two-axle buses built to this length to operate anywhere in the United Kingdom under special dispensation from the Ministry of Transport. By 1956, most motorbus manufacturers were starting production of 30ft-long double-deckers on two axles. They were not good-looking vehicles (especially from the front) and were given the nickname 'Goldfish Bowls'. No. 864 was one of the original fifteen Sunbeam F4As and today is preserved at the Sandtoft Transport Centre at Sandtoft near Doncaster.

(P. J. Thompson)

Opposite, top: Loading up in St Paul's Street at the corrugated iron-roofed bus shelters is Roe-bodied Sunbeam W4 332, (JDH 433). This semi-utility-bodied trolleybus had entered service on 11 February 1946 and would remain in use until New Year's Eve 1965. At this time, in about 1950, there were still only two trolleybus routes in Walsall; it is not long after the No. 30 route was redirected into the town centre by way of St Paul's Street, rather than Park Street. The trolleybus would pull away from the shadow of St Paul's Church and would proceed on to the original terminus at The Bridge.

(R. Hannay)

Below: Looking across St Paul's Street from the corner of Darwell Street shows the 1935 brick-built Central Bus Station when it was about fifteen years old. Standing at the shelters alongside St Paul's Church is 1931-built Sunbeam MS2 163, (ADH 9). This trolleybus had a Short Brothers body which was among the last bodies built on trolleybus chassis by this Rochester-based bodybuilder. The trolleybus is still carrying its original fleet number as for its last year in service it was allocated the fleet number 309.

(D. R. Harvey Collection)

No. 877, (GFU 695), started life as Cleethorpes Corporation 164 and had a BUT 9611T chassis and was fitted with a Northern Coachbuilders H28/26R body. When built these NCB bodies belonged to the last design type produced by this Newcastle-based bodybuilder. Looking very similar to the contemporary ECW body, these four were the only bodies of this style to be mounted on trolleybus chassis. Soon after purchase, three of the four BUTs were lengthened to 30ft long and rebuilt to forward entrance configuration with an H37/30F layout. No. 877 is at the bottom of St Paul's Street with Darwall Street behind the turning trolleybus.

(D. R. Harvey Collection)

The view up the hill in St Paul's Street one dark evening in 1966 shows the bus station above the row of trolleybuses on the left, the distant premises of Dean's wholesale warehouse and the impressive head offices of the Transport Department – the clock tower showing 6.05pm – which were first occupied in July 1935. The layout of the overhead in St Paul's Street is clearly shown with the two inbound overhead wires leading into the tight 180° turn at the junction with Darwall Street. On the left is No. 858, (TDH 908), one of the 30ft long Willowbrook-bodied Sunbeam F4A, while in front of it is the only motorbus in the queue, No. 230, (ODH 307), a 1951 Guy 'Arab' III 6LW with a full-fronted Park Royal body which has its sliding cab door open. The front two trolleybuses are No. 863, (TDH 913), another Sunbeam F4A, 340, (NDH 957), and travelling up St Paul's Street on the No. 31 route to Mossley, having just pulled away from the top loading shelter is No. 346, (ADX 195), one of the former Ipswich vehicles.

(H. F. Wheeller Collection)

Standing in the distant shadow of the Marks & Spencer and F.W. Woolworth shops in Park Street, which backed on to St Paul's Bus Station, is No. 322, (JDH 29). This trolleybus was originally numbered 225 and was the first wartime trolleybus to be allocated to Walsall by the Ministry of War Transport. The Park Royal body of this Sunbeam F4 could be easily distinguished by the slope at the bottom of the front cab-side window. In addition, the thick upper saloon body pillar is identifiable and it was within a conduit in this pillar that the wiring from the overhead to the motors was carried.

(R. Marshall Collection)

Waiting to leave Walsall Bus Station on the 32 to Lower Farm on 26 June 1963 is 344, (ADX 193). This former Ipswich Corporation, Park Royal-bodied Sunbeam F4 entered service on 9 April 1962 and would normally be found employed on the joint Walsall to Wolverhampton service at this time having been purchased to augment the Walsall fleet on the latter route. The Sunbeam F4A trolleybus in front has had its poles taken down so the driver of No. 344 would have had to really pull very hard to the right in order to clear the parked trolleybus. Behind the bus station is the distant Bridge area of the town with the 1935 George Hotel block just visible.

(W. Ryan)

The only six-wheel trolleybus to be purchased in post-war years was No. 850, (RDH 990). It is standing at the bus shelters in St Paul's Bus Station when working on the No. 30 route to Leamore. Delivered in September 1953 this Sunbeam S7 was 30ft long and 8ft wide. No. 850 had a Willowbrook H38/24D body with an extra capacity for fifteen standees on the rear of the lower saloon. It was designed as one of Edgley Cox's first trolleybus experiments with a conductor's desk on the rear platform. No. 850 originally had a centre staircase and a centre exit door in the middle of the lower saloon. It was rebuilt to an H36/27RD layout in February 1961 when it was renumbered 350. This trolleybus, known because of its size as the 'Queen Mary', was never a popular bus either with drivers or conductors. Other than the NDH-registered trolleybuses, No. 850 was the only other Walsall trolleybus to have a sliding cab door.

(J. Bishop)

Even in the days when trolleybuses ruled the Bloxwich services, occasional motorbuses were used on the 30 route. Here No. 821, (TDH 673), the lightweight Northern Counties H37/28R bodied Daimler CVG5, which had been exhibited at the 1954 Commercial Motor Show, leaves the bus station when there is nothing else in St Paul's other than Sunbeam F4A trolleybuses.

(D. R. Harvey Collection)

Loading up at Platform 4 in Walsall's St Paul's Bus Station in about 1964 is one of the 30ft-long 'Goldfish Bowls'. These buses were also known as 'Liners'. No. 861 (TDH 911), a Sunbeam F4A with a Willowbrook H36/34R body is working on the No. 32 service to Lower Farm Estate. The Walsall trolleybuses at this time were in their pomp and despite the ugly frontal design, they were smartly turned out. The cars parked alongside St Paul's Church are a Ford Anglia 105E and a four-door Ford Consul Classic 116E.

(A. J. Douglas)

Pulling away from the stand at the top end of platform 3, leaving for Bloxwich on the No. 30 route, is trolleybus 320, (HDH 213). After 1955, the 15 service was the only trolleybus route to use one of the inner bus station platforms while the No. 30 service continued to use platform 4. The trolleybus is nearing the end of its working life and is wearing the over all-blue livery introduced by the new General Manager Mr Edgley Cox in 1952. The vehicle is one of the four Sunbeam MS2s which entered service on 1 March 1940. The Park Royal H32/28R bodies on these trolleybuses were based on contemporary vehicles being supplied to Huddersfield Corporation. Although this date was six months after the outbreak of the Second World War their bodies were built to full pre-war standards.

(R. A. Mills)

The much-rebuilt 342 (NDH 959) sets off from St Paul's Bus Station when on its way to Bloxwich on the No. 30 route in the last month of trolleybus operation. It is sandwiched between 2592, (JOJ 592), a former Birmingham City Transport Guy 'Arab' III Special with a Metro-Cammell H30/24R body, working on the No. 31 route to the Mossley Estate and a brand new WMPTE NCME-bodied Daimler 'Fleetline' CRG6LX 4022, (VOH 22J), which had entered service in August 1970 having been ordered originally by Walsall Corporation. No. 342 had been withdrawn in April 1960 for experimental purposes. It was lengthened to 30ft using Dennis 'Loline' chassis frames and re-seated to H34/31R, but it only went back into regular service in May 1967. It is now preserved at the Sandtoft Trolleybus Museum.

(L. Mason)

There were only sixty-one post-war Crossley TDD42 trolleybus chassis constructed, and the two delivered in 1951 to Cleethorpes Corporation in February 1951 were not only the only ones to be attractively bodied by Charles Roe but were also the last two to be constructed. No. 850, (HBE 541) was the first of the two TDD42/3s to enter service in February 1961 and survived in service until February 1970 under the first tranche of trolleybus withdrawals undertaken by WMPTE. It is leaving St Paul's Bus Station not long after it entered service and is working on the shortworking to Leamore. No. 850 is passing the still unoccupied row of 1968-built shops which had replaced the early nineteenth-century buildings around St Paul's Close. These shops just beyond the church have now disappeared under the controversial futuristic bus station opened on 2 August 2001.

(D. R. Harvey Collection)

Leaving St Paul's Bus Station on 24 July 1963 is 875, (GFU 693), when the nineteenth-century buildings near to the inbound unloading point were still in use. This was the first of the three former Cleethorpes Corporation BUT 9611Ts which were lengthened to 30ft. The rebuilt bus had its seating capacity increased by thirteen to sixty-nine and converted to having a forward entrance layout. The rebuilding of the NCB body was done very sympathetically, and while the extra weight of the lengthened body was considerable the 115hp Metro-Vick motor could cope quite comfortably. The staff sometimes referred to the three rebuilt buses as 'Tankers'.

(D. R. Harvey Collection)

The old order passes the new order in St Paul's Street. 352, (ADX 190), one of the former Ipswich Corporation Sunbeam F4s with Park Royal H30/26R bodies, overtakes one of the short-length NCME-bodied rear-engined Daimler 'Fleetline' CRG6LWs which is parked alongside the Transport Department offices. No. 27, (BDH 427C), dated from January 1965, and with its flat-front and deep windscreen perhaps looks more like a trolleybus than a motorbus. No. 352 is working on the 15 circular route to Blakenall and Bloxwich in about 1968. It is noticeable that all the other five trolleybuses standing in the bus station are the larger 30ft-long, Willowbrook-bodied Sunbeam F4As.

(J. Saunders)

Chapter Four

THROUGH BIRCHILLS AND LEAMORE TO BLOXWICH

At first sight, Bloxwich appears to be little more than a suburb of Walsall, but for generations dating back to Anglo-Saxon times it had been a settlement in its own right. The town stands on the northern edge of the West Midlands conurbation and historically marked the boundary between the rural agricultural landscape of Staffordshire and the coal mining that developed in the eighteenth century. The original centre was probably at the southern end of the present High Street in the Pinfold area, with building spreading north as encroachment on the wasteland. The streets between Elmore Green Road and New Street apparently date from the later 1870s. Wolverhampton Street had been cut by 1879 when the first of several terraces was built there. The local canal was developed in the early nineteenth century to transport raw materials and heavy iron products while the opening of the railway station in 1858 encouraged the growth of the town. Bloxwich became an important point on the route between Walsall and Stafford when the turnpiking of Stafford Road took place in 1766. This road is the present day A34 and passes Birchills garage and passes through Leamore.

This chapter examines the 'mainline' 30 route through Leamore into Bloxwich. This was the second of Walsall's trolleybus routes to be opened. Other than the change of the town terminus the rest of the route survived largely unaltered throughout its operational life. A separate chapter looks at the circular route extension through Blakenall.

In 1969, just weeks before control of the Walsall municipal bus and trolleybus fleet was taken over on 1 October, the rebuilt 'Goldfish Bowl' turns from the distant St Paul's Street into Wisemore as it makes its way towards Stafford Street. The trolleybus is working on the No. 31 route to Mossley and is loaded to the gunwales with passengers. The trolleybus is No. 866, (XDH 66), and perhaps might have been the first of all of these trolleybuses to be converted. Unfortunately, just like the attempt to purchase all the remaining Bournemouth Sunbeam MF2 trolleybuses, Mr Cox's efforts were admirable but too late as the PTE's intention was to get rid of the Walsall trolleybuses as quickly as possible.

(D. R. Harvey Collection)

Turning into Stafford Street, to the right of the distinctive Richmond's kitchenware store, on its way to Bloxwich by way of Leamore is No. 858, (TDH 908). The twenty-two Willowbrook-bodied seventy-seat Sunbeam F4As were the trolleybuses of choice on the Bloxwich service for most of their working lives and even in WMPTE days they were being worked hard on this busy route.

(R. Symons)

Carrying a full load of passengers, Willowbrook-bodied Sunbeam F4A 852, (TDH 902), turns left into Wisemore in the shadow of Deans Wholesale Warehouse from Stafford Street. The trolleybus is working on an inbound No. 31 service from Mossley. The public house in the distance on the left in Stafford Street alongside the Morris Minor 1000 is the Cuckoo Bell. This part of the street is still lined with nineteenth-century retail premises.

(D. R. Harvey Collection)

One of the three rebuilt former-Cleethorpes double-decker BUT 9611Ts, No. 875, (GFU 693), has passed the distant tower of St Peter's Church in Stafford Street and is about to cross the junction with Portland Street on its way into Walsall on the 33 circular service. In 1967 a new one-way traffic system was introduced in the centre of Walsall and as part of this scheme a section of Stafford Street was to be one-way except for buses. All other traffic had to turn left following the signs for the A34 but this 'cut through' did allow the Corporation's vehicles to get direct access to Wisemore and Park Street. The trolleybus had been rebuilt to a forward entrance, 30ft-long, sixty-nine-seater, which gave it a comparable capacity to the Willowbrook-bodied Sunbeam F4As.

(J. Saunders)

The 32 route to the Lower Farm Estate was introduced on 31 December 1962. It was the penultimate trolleybus service to open and was an extension beyond Bloxwich, having followed the original 30 service. Returning into the town in Stafford Street is numerically Walsall's highest numbered trolleybus. No. 877, (GFU 695), has come past the trees on the corner of Proffitt Street on the right where the anti-clockwise No. 15 route to Blakenall turned off the northern end of Stafford Street. On the right, beyond the Ford Thames 300E van converted into an estate car, is the half-timbered Royal Exchange public house.

(R. F. Mack)

A Ford 300E Thames 5cwt van waits in Croft Street for the trolleybus to pass on its outward journey along Stafford Street. No. 340, (NDH 957), approaches Proffitt Street when working on the 32 route to Lower Farm. This Sunbeam F4 had a Brush H30/26R body and entered service on 1 November 1951, just in time to replace the Beadle and Short-bodied Sunbeam MS2s built in 1933. Towering above the trolleybus is St Peter's Church, which is half hidden by the advertising hoarding for Benson & Hedges cigarettes.

(R. Symons)

In Bloxwich Road, travelling towards Walsall town centre as it passes Hospital Street on 4 May 2009, is Volvo B10L 1473, (R473 XDA), fitted with a Wright B43F body. It is working on the 301 route and is painted in the red and white National Express corporate livery. The bus is approaching Proffitt Street where the circular 15 service turned off Bloxwich Road on its way to Blakenall.

(D. R. Harvey)

Having crossed over Pratt's Bridge above the Wyrley & Essington Canal, No. 854, (TDH 904), speeds along Bloxwich Road when working on the 31 route to the Mossley Estate. The Willowbrook bodies on these large Sunbeam F4As were fitted with doors, although in this case it was running with the doors open. This must have added quite considerably to the noise when these trolleybuses were in service as their lightweight bodies were not exactly the most robust and did tend to vibrate and clatter quite a lot and when coupled with the rattling of the doors could make for an uncomfortably noisy ride.

(D. R. Harvey Collection)

The order by West Midlands PTE for 200 Bristol VRT/SL6Gs with MCW H43/33F bodywork was something of a surprise and all of these were allocated either to Birchills garage or Park Lane garage in Wolverhampton. No. 4357, (EOF 357L), has just passed Carl Street which led to Birchills garage. It is about to travel along this section of Birchills Road, which was lined by the late 1880s Victorian terraced housing locally known as Depot Row. This Bristol VRT is working on the No. 333 route circular, the successor to the 33 trolleybus route to Bloxwich and Leamore on 26 August 1984.

(D. R. Harvey)

Turning into Birchills depot's southern entrance at Carl Street for the last time on Sunday 3 October 1970 is the much-rebuilt No. 342, (NDH 959). It has worked on the last enthusiasts' tour around the trolleybus routes before the last three trolleybuses (Sunbeam F4As 862, 864 and 872) would ceremonially close the Walsall system. These three vehicles and No. 342 are all preserved. No. 342 had been extended to 30ft long by enlarging the wheelbase to 18ft 6in using Dennis 'Loline' frames. The trolleybus was out of use for seven years, being rebuilt before it returned to service.

(C. W. Routh)

Just pulling away from the trolleybus stop outside the large gabled offices of the Transport Department at Birchills garage in Bloxwich Road is No. 158, (ADH 4). These offices were built in June 1885 when the depot was opened by the South Staffordshire Tramways Company for the Bloxwich steam tram service. It is working on the Bloxwich service but is showing the 28 destination number which Walsall had used for the turn backs at Willenhall in earlier days. No. 158 was one of the five Beadle-bodied Sunbeam MS2s of 1933 and is still wearing its semi-streamlined livery on the lower side panels. It was renumbered as 305 in October 1950. Trailing away behind the trolleybus is the Depot Row terrace of 1890s housing.

(D. R. Harvey Collection)

Speeding along Bloxwich Road on the No. 31 route is No. 870, (XDH 70). This Willowbrook-bodied Sunbeam F4A is travelling towards the town centre and is passing the 1920s semi-detached housing opposite Birchills depot. The long straight stretches along Bloxwich Road were really suited to these seventy seaters although, perhaps surprisingly, they were fitted with quite small 95hp Metro-Vick motors. By comparison, the contemporary Glasgow BUT 9613T trolleybuses had 125hp motors.

(Travel Lens)

The Walsall trolleybuses were never repainted into WMPTE livery, but the only obvious alteration was the painting out of the Walsall municipal crests and the legal ownership lettering. No. 868, (XDH 68), is passing the northern entrance to Birchills depot. In the background are the Victorian houses near Beeches Road. The first fifteen Sunbeam F4As were purchased for the opening of the new trolleybus service to Blakenall in 1955 and the last seven, of which No. 868 was one, were bought for the opening of a new trolleybus service to Beechdale and also to replace the last of the pre-war, three-axle trolleybuses.

(D. R. Harvey Collection)

Standing opposite Birchills depot in 1936 is Short-bodied Sunbeam MS2 161, (ADH 7). The trolleybus is painted in the attractive gold-lined out light blue and cream livery. It is working towards Walsall from Bloxwich on the No. 30 service which at this time was still only the second trolleybus route. These 1933-vintage vehicles were the last trolleybus bodies constructed by Shorts Brothers who stopped building bus bodies in 1935.

(D. R. Harvey)

Approaching Birchills depot from the north with the entrance to Beatrice Street behind it on the left, No. 862, (TDH 912), passes an advertising hoarding carrying advertisements for Cadbury's Whole Nut chocolate bars and Haig's whisky. Following the trolleybus is a Standard Eight saloon. This Sunbeam F4A appears to be returning to Birchills depot as the driver has his hand through the signalling window and the destination blind still shows the trolleybus working on the 30 route to Bloxwich. No. 862 is currently the only active member of the class and is a regular performer at the Black Country Living Museum in Dudley where it is beautifully restored.

(L. Mason)

Walsall operated their driver training trolleybuses without passengers whereas some other trolleybus operators ran their trainee vehicles in service. Here, No. 334, (NDE 953), one of the Brush-bodied Sunbeam F4s, travels along Bloxwich Road with the distant junction of Webster Road and Forest Lane behind the distant trolleybus. It is passing the My Cellar outdoor with its very 1960s-styled sign over the shop.

(D. R. Harvey Collection)

Formerly Cleethorpes Corporation 63, No. 850 was acquired by Walsall in July 1960 as the first of the pair of Crossley TDD42/3s with Metro-Vick 95hp motors and fitted with attractive Roe H29/25R bodies. The trolleybus has passed the Rosum Cinema in Leamore as it travels back towards Birchills depot when on driver training duties. The cinema is behind the trolleybus beyond the junction with Leamore Lane. On the other corner, off the photograph, in Harden Road is the Butlers Arms public house which closed in 2008. This crossroads had been intended for a new trolleybus route from Leamore Lane where it would link with the 33 route to the Royal Oak public house in Blakenall on the No. 15 route. Despite having powers to build and operate this connecting route, Walsall Corporation never built it.

(R. F. Mack)

The only turnback on the 30 route to Bloxwich was at the Red Lion public house. The throat of the Green Lane junction with Bloxwich Road was sufficiently wide to allow for an overhead loop for outbound trolleybuses to return to Walsall. The driver of six-wheeler No. 320, formerly 218, (HDH 213), one of the four Sunbeam MS2s built in 1940 with rather stylish Park Royal bodies, waits for No. 342, (NDH 959), to pass on its way back to Bloxwich depot. No. 342, of course, was the subject of a seven-year rebuilding into a 30ft-long vehicle. Both trolleybuses are in the Somerfield-era light blue livery with dark blue bands.

(C. W. Routh)

Above: Sunbeam F4A trolleybus 854, (TDH 904), begins to make its way into Bloxwich Road's gentle gradient as it leaves Bloxwich for Leamore just over ½ mile away. The smartly painted Willowbrook-bodied trolleybus has come from the Mossley Estate on the 31 service. On the right are the last of the Victorian terraced houses that survived the 1960s redevelopment near to the Pinfold. Behind the trolleybus and the almost new Austin Cambridge of 1964 is the local Bloxwich health centre.

(R. F. Mack)

Opposite, top: The tower of All Saints' parish church stands against the skyline behind Sunbeam MS2 871, (TDH 71), which is standing in High Street just to the south of the junction with Elmore Green Road. The trolleybus is working back to Walsall on the 31 service, which, despite the destination display, has come from the Mossley Estate. The main body of the church dated from about 1791 but this west tower, with its pyramid roof and stumpy pinnacles was added by 1877.

(Omnicolour)

Below: No. 851, (TDH 901), the first of the ground-breaking, 30ft-long, two-axled Sunbeam F4As that was the only one of the batch to have entered service in 1954, travels out of Bloxwich along the High Street. It is on its way towards Walsall on the circular 15 route, the trolleybus is near St Peter's Roman Catholic church on the right, while opposite is the still fairly new Woolworth's shop on the corner of New Street. On the left, next to the George Hotel, the new premises of Midland Bank are still under construction.

(D. R. Harvey Collection)

Above: Travelling towards the nearby turning loop in High Street, Bloxwich is Sunbeam F4A 857, (TDH 907). This vehicle is working on the clockwise No. 30 route to Blakenall. Standing at the top shelter in High Street just before the angled junction with Park Road is No. 872, (XDH 72), the last of these Willowbrook-bodied four-wheelers. This trolleybus is being employed on the anti-clockwise circular 15 service back to Walsall by way of Bloxwich Road.

(D. R. Harvey Collection)

Opposite, top: Coming out of Wolverhampton Road, Bloxwich in front of the old Music Hall building is 852, (TDH 902), which is working on the 33 service from the Dudley Fields Estate. This route did have an identity crisis, as trolleybuses seemed to display arbitrarily 'Circular via Beechdale Estate', 'Circular via Dudley Fields Estate' or even just 'Cavendish Road'. The trolleybus is about to turn right into the High Street where it will gain its bus stop opposite the ornamental Promenade Gardens.

(Travel Lens Photographic)

Below: Just pulling away from the bus shop in High Street, Bloxwich is rebuilt and extended No. 875, (GFU 693). This BUT 9611T is working on the 15 route and has come from Blakenall on its way back towards Walsall. Coming out of Wolverhampton Street is a Corporation motorbus while behind it is the old music hall building, built in 1857. During the Depression it became the Labour Exchange and is currently a sports hall.

(C. Carter)

Passing the old music hall building in High Street, Bloxwich with the gable end of the cycle shop on the corner of Wolverhampton Street behind it is No. 153, (DH 8313). This Guy BTX six-wheeler had a Brush H32/28R body and is seen during the Second World War. The unusual ventilators in the lower saloon were not repeated on the subsequent 1933 deliveries. The trolleybus has a somewhat battered lower offside front panel around the masked headlight, while the rather tired-looking paintwork had been added to by having all the lower edges marked out in white paint to help identify the vehicle in the blackout. Originally, No. 153 was going to be numbered 9 but after delivery it was given this new fleet number. These Guy BTXs were built, along with the pair of AEC 663Ts, for the opening of the joint Wolverhampton 29 service. They had Rees-Roturbo 60hp regenerative motors that put power back into the overhead when the trolleybus was braking, and this became standard for all subsequent pre-war Walsall trolleybuses.

(D. R. Harvey Collection)

Parked in High Street is Brush-bodied Sunbeam F4 339, (NDH 956). It is standing in the lay-by alongside the former Bloxwich Music Hall building and is working on the 32 route to Lower Farm Estate in about 1963. It is surprising that at this late stage the trolleybus is still looking in fairly original condition with an all light blue livery with thin black beading. Next door to the old musical hall building is Bloxwich C of E Junior and Infant school, which was opened as a National School in 1862.

(2489 Group)

The M&B Bulls Head public house was closed in 2008 but until recently it was one of the more popular public houses in Bloxwich. Standing in Park Road, this 1938-built public house overlooked the loading up trolleybus stop at the top end of the Promenade Gardens in High Street. The trolleybus is No. 874, (GFU 692), a 1950 NCB-bodied BUT 9611T which is working on the 15 service from Blakenall and is parked outside the 1950s public toilets. No. 874 was formerly owned by Cleethorpes Corporation which re-entered service in Walsall in February 1962. It was the only one of the four BUTs purchased from the Lincolnshire municipal operator not to be extended and converted to forward entrance and is preserved at Sandtoft where it will ultimately be restored as Grimsby-Cleethorpes 161.

(M. Rooum)

Wearing a rather faded pre-war livery is the second of the pair of 1938-vintage Park Royal-bodied Sunbeam MS2. No. 188, (EDH 864), entered service on 28 February 1938 and would remain in service until July 1956. It is pictured here before it was renumbered 317 in October 1950. This 80hp-motored sixty seater is moving past the Promenade Gardens. It has left the original terminus of the No. 30 route, which prior to 1955 was opposite the Bell Inn at the junction of Lichfield Road.

(S. N. J. White)

The Bell Inn was the turning circle for the original 30 route at the northern end of the High Street, Bloxwich. No. 318, (HDH 213), was one of the last of the pre-war six-wheelers to enter the Walsall fleet in March 1940. This Sunbeam MS2 had a Park Royal H32/28R body and had just been renumbered as it waits to pull away from the pub yard in November 1950. Within a few days this turning loop would be replaced by the loop going right off the High Street and moving anticlockwise around the Ornamental Gardens before terminating opposite the Bell Inn.

(J. S. Webb)

No. 342, (NDH 959), passes the ornamental Promenade Gardens in High Street, Bloxwich and turns into Park Road in order to negotiate the later turning loop on the last day of trolleybus operation in Walsall on 3 October 1970. Behind the trolleybus is a former Birmingham City Transport Guy 'Arab' III Special with a Metro-Cammell H30/24R body dating from 1950. The drafting in of these buses caused a lot of resentment in Walsall, as they were generally considerably older than the trolleybuses they were replacing!

(D. Johnson)

Negotiating the loop in Park Road, Bloxwich around the eastern side of the Promenade Gardens on 18 June 1951 is No. 321, (HDH 214), one of the 1940-vintage, Park Royal-bodied Sunbeam MS2s, which had only been renumbered from 219 in October of the previous year. Prior to that, the trolleybus fleet numbers had been in an ascending discontinuous sequence starting in 1931 at No. 151 and ending in 1946 with No. 237, the last of the wartime four-wheelers. The trolleybus is slowly being taken back to the High Street in Bloxwich before returning to Walsall.

(J. S. Webb)

Standing at the original inbound terminus of the No. 30 trolleybus route at the north end of High Street opposite the Bell Hotel is No. 329, (JDH 334). It is July 1951 and this wartime Sunbeam W4, fitted with a Brush 'utility' body waits in High Street and is standing in front of one of Weymann-bodied Sunbeam MS2s of 1933 which had just been repainted into the all-over light blue livery. Although renumbered from 233 in October 1950, this wartime trolleybus is still painted in the dark and light blue wartime livery. On the right is a wartime Guy 'Arab' II working into Bloxwich along Lichfield Road.

(D. F. Parker)

Above: The driver of the six-wheeler is about to get back into his cab before leaving for the return journey to Walsall. It is standing alongside the concrete bus shelters at the far end of the High Street opposite the Bell Hotel in about 1952. The overlap between the entrance into service of the almost new No. 343, (NDH 960), and the pre-war Weymann-bodied six-wheel Sunbeam MS2 311, (ADH 11), standing in front of it was only just over four years. Both trolleybuses are waiting to return to Walsall on the original 30 route.

(C. W. Routh)

Opposite, top: During the Second World War it wasn't just the vehicles that had blackout paintwork but also the street furniture and even the trees! Life during the Second World War is frequently portrayed as long, dark days of gloom and austerity. What is often forgotten is that life went on as normal when the sun still shone, people carried on living their lives and the trees carried on growing. On one such day, No. 218, (HDH 213), stands at the north end of High Street, Bloxwich when wearing headlight masks and white blackout edgings.

(J. S. Webb)

Below: Standing at the northern end of High Street, Bloxwich is one of the two Bournemouth trolleybuses lent to Walsall Corporation during the Second World War. No. 79, (AEL 407), was on loan from 1 June 1943 and was returned to the south coast resort on 17 July 1945, having previously been on loan to South Shields Corporation. While the Sunbeam MS2 chassis of this pair were the same as most of the Walsall six-wheelers, the English Electric bodies were very different, with two doors and two staircases. The front doors were not used in their time in Walsall.

(J. S. Webb)

No. 324, (JDH 331), was one of four Brush-bodied Sunbeam W4s delivered in the late spring of 1945. Looking very smart, this trolleybus is still in the two-tone blue livery. No. 324 is leaving Lichfield Road, formerly known as Little Bloxwich Lane and is turning into High Street before returning to the trolleybus stop at the terminus in the centre of Bloxwich. It is working on the 15 service from Blakenall, the first of the added loops which R. Edgley Cox inaugurated.

(C. W. Routh)

CHAPTER FIVE

BLAKENALL HEATH

The post-war enlargement of the Walsall trolleybus system really began with the opening of the route through Blakenall Heath. Various plans had been proposed to enlarge the original existing system of the No. 29 route to Willenhall and later to Wolverhampton and the No. 30 route to Bloxwich along Bloxwich Road through Leamore. The most disappointing was the failure in 1937 to obtain local authority permission to operate trolleybuses on the Walsall-Darlaston-Wednesbury circular services that were numbered as motorbus services, 37 and 38.

The gaining of the Walsall Corporation (Trolley Vehicles) Order Confirmation Act in 1953 gave Mr R. Edgley Cox, the new Walsall Corporation general manager, the opportunity to enlarge the trolleybus services into the new housing estates. These had been developing to the north of the town since the early 1920s. The first tangible evidence that the trolleybus system was going to be enlarged was the opening of a new trolleybus garage on 7 October 1954.

The first of these new trolleybus extensions took place on 6 June 1955, using the top of Platform 3 in the bus station, by which time all of the first fifteen of the 30ft-long, two-axled Sunbeam F4As had been delivered enabling the new extensions to be implemented. The new route was the 15 service to Blakenall Heath. This was further enlarged on 10 October 1955 from Blakenall to Bloxwich, which enabled a circular service to be introduced. The clockwise route from Walsall, via Leamore to Bloxwich and then on to Blakenall before returning to Walsall became the 30 route, and the anticlockwise service was the newly introduced 15 route. Irrespective of whether the shortworkings went to either Bloxwich or Blakenall, once a shortworking had reached its terminus it turned back, but retained its original route number! Strangely, the trolleybus destination blinds made much more of the fact that it was a circular service and always showed Blakenall rather than the more accurate Blakenall Heath. The Blakenall service left Bloxwich by way of Lichfield Road through an already established area of owner-occupied housing before reaching the council-built housing at the heart of the area at Blakenall Heath where the Early English-styled Christ Church stands behind its stout churchyard wall.

Blakenall Heath was originally a rural area north of Walsall, but the area changed dramatically between 1918 and 1939. Farmland gave way to council housing, surrounding the local church and the surviving eighteenth- and nineteenth-century farm buildings. Walsall Borough's first council house was built in Blakenall Heath, on Blakenall Lane, during June 1920. Within seven years, 500 council houses had been built in the area and by 1939 more than 1,000 had been built. Following the end of the Second World War further housing developments took place over the next thirty years. It was into this area that Mr Cox realised that there would be a valuable new market for trolleybus services radiating from the Bloxwich area. The trolleybus services in the area were extended in the 1950s and early 1960s to the developing housing estates at Dudley Fields, Mossley and Lower Farm in the Bloxwich area as the system finally stabilised to a route mileage of 12.69 miles. All the Bloxwich trolleybus services lasted until the final closure on 3 October 1970.

This chapter looks only at the 1955 extension from Bloxwich Road through Blakenall and on to Bloxwich as the Bloxwich Lane service through Leamore is dealt with in the previous section.

The Blakenall circular trolleybus service was introduced on 6 June 1955 with the original 30 route going to Bloxwich and then taking a clockwise route through Blakenall and back onto Bloxwich Lane at its junction with Stafford Street. A council estate was built to the north of Proffitt Street, and in the 1930s the corporation rebuilt the Victorian slums in the old streets to the south. The No. 15 service ran in the opposite direction from Walsall through Blakenall to Bloxwich. No. 353, (ADX 191), one of the eight Ipswich Corporation Sunbeam F4s with a Park Royal H30/26R body, is in Proffitt Street near Leckie Road when working on the No. 30 service near to the Bloxwich Road/ Stafford Street junction in about 1964.

(R. F. Mack)

Travelling over the bridge across the former LNWR railway line in Coalpool Lane, Ryecroft is No. 851, (TDH 901). This Willowbrook-bodied Sunbeam F4A is working on the 15 service down the hill towards the cemetery. In the distance is the power station owned by the Midlands Electricity Board built near the site of Birchills' first blast furnace during 1948 and 1949. Cooling towers, a new generating station, railway sidings and a canal basin were constructed to facilitate the plant. However, within decades this became obsolete and was closed down.

(D. R. Harvey Collection)

When it was first new, No. 851, (TDH 901), was exhibited at the 1954 Commercial Motor Show where it was the first ever 30ft long double-decker bus on two axles. It was a genuinely historic vehicle as it trailed the way towards the 1956 changes in the Construction & Use Regulations. This allowed the introduction of longer motorbuses such as the Leyland 'Titan' PD3, the Daimler CVG6/30, the Dennis 'Loline' Mk I and the stretched versions of the AEC 'Regent' V. It was perhaps no coincidence that Walsall was an early purchaser of varieties of the last three types. By the early 1960s, No. 851 was just another 'Goldfish Bowl' Willowbrook-bodied Sunbeam F4A as it passed the entrance to the main gates of Ryecroft Cemetery.

(D. R. Harvey Collection)

Travelling towards Blakenall on the 15 service is, yet again, No. 851, (TDH 901). It is passing Ryecroft Cemetery in Coalpool Lane, which was opened in 1894, where it is inching past TXV 906, being employed on some overhead maintenance work. This is an AEC 'Mercury' Mk II with an Eagle built tower wagon that had been built for London Transport in July 1958, where it was numbered 1073Q. It was acquired in May 1962 immediately after the closure of London's trolleybus system and was transferred to WMPTE in October 1969.

(D. R. Harvey Collection)

Above: On its way towards Ryecroft Cemetery as it heads towards Walsall on the 15 service from Blakenall is Sunbeam F4A 857, (TDH 907). This Willowbrook-bodied trolleybus has just travelled along Ross Road from the right as it passes Coalpool Place in the heart of the Blakenall Estate. The trolleybus has just left the right turn at the traffic island at the junction with Harden Road. This junction was within half a mile of the main A461 Lichfield Road at Rushall. The large Coalpool council estate was built in the late 1920s to the west of Coalpool Lane and it was extended northwards to Forest Lane. Trolleybuses seemed to have two types of natural suburban landscapes, either speeding along concrete-sectioned roadways or, as in this case, through a municipal housing area.

(R. F. Mack)

Opposite, top: Climbing up Harden Road up the valley side of the Ford Brook is Willowbrook-bodied Sunbeam F4A 857, (TDH 907). It is working on the 15 route in Harden Road near Coalpool Bridge when travelling north-westwards towards Blakenall and Bloxwich. On the left is the Harden area of parkland of which the Wyrley & Essington Canal forms the northern edge. Shortly the trolleybus will reach the bridge over this canal and its extension opened throughout by 1797.

(D. R. Harvey Collection)

Below: Trolleybuses always made little of steep hills on their routes and so No. 868, (XDH 68), is able to power its way up Harden Road near to the Edgar Stammers Junior and Infant School. This was the steepest hill on the Walsall trolleybus system. Outside the school is the obligatory 'lollipop' man. On the right is the bridge wall of the Coalpool Canal Bridge over the Wyrley & Essington Canal. This canal was built through the area in the 1790s and was affectionately known as the 'Curly Wyrley' because it is a contour canal. This type of canal follows the land contours as it twists and turns in order to avoid any gradients and thus the need for locks. The trolleybus is being followed by a Ford Anglia 105E saloon.

(R. F. Mack)

On a day in January 1964 when the snow is still just about hanging on, a salt-and-mud-splattered Sunbeam F4A trolleybus No. 864, (TDH 914), hurries along Walker Road when working on the 15 route from Walsall. The trolleybus is passing some of the late nineteenth-century villas which began the slow suburbanisation of this part of northern Walsall.

(D. F. Parker)

The driver of Sunbeam F4A trolleybus No. 871, (XDH 71), talks to the inspector as they stand by the vehicle alongside the Victorian Christ Church at Blakenall Heath. The trolleybus is parked in the northbound loading lane facing Ryecroft and Walsall on the 30 route. The trolleybuses were wired to travel along both sides of the church as well as there being a turning loop on the Ingram Road side of the parish church which No. 871 will use in order to turn round. In the background, another of the same type, No. 863, (TDH 913), is about to leave for Bloxwich on the 15 service.

(A. B. Cross)

Parked in Blakenall in sight of Christ Church, is former Grimsby-Cleethorpes trolleybus 874, (GFU 692). The trolleybus is facing the Walker Road side of the circular service and is showing Leamore on the destination blind. This NCB-bodied BUT 9611T was the only one of the four of the type not to be substantially rebuilt by Walsall which probably accounts for its survival in preservation. No. 874 is waiting in the narrow one-way bus lane used by trolleybuses travelling back towards Walsall. Christ Church cost about £5,000 to build and was completed and in use by 1870, although it was not consecrated until 1872. The distinctive tower was not completed until 1882. When it was built the church was virtually on its own on the local heath-land although the cottages in the distance on the left which also appear in the previous photograph pre-date the church by well over half a century.

(D. R. Harvey Collection)

Drifting into Walker Road as it leaves the trolleybus turning loop to the north of Blakenall church's graveyard is another of the ubiquitous Sunbeam F4As. No. 870, (XDH 70), was one of the extra seven of these Willowbrook-bodied trolleybuses delivered in October 1956. In the background are some of the 1,000-plus inter-war council houses, but alongside the trolleybus is one of the few pre-Victorian rows of farm workers' cottages to survive the building of the twentieth-century housing estates in the Blakenall area. The journey time between Blakenall Church and Walsall was just sixteen minutes. The normal daytime service was about every fifteen to twenty minutes around the circular route, though there was always a shortworking between Walsall and Blakenall running between each of the circulars.

(R. F. Mack)

Passing the multi-storey flats in Blakenall Lane is Roe-bodied Crossley TDD42/3 trolleybus No. 850, (HBE 541). This trolleybus had been Grimsby-Cleethorpes Transport's 163 which had originally entered service in February 1951. Crossley trolleybuses had notoriously heavy steering and so, if true to form, this is why Nos. 850 and 873 were underused in their years with Walsall. The only other trolleybuses fitted with this style of Roe bodywork were Bradford Corporation's 740-751 of 1949, which were mounted on BUT 9611T chassis. It is May 1961 – some three months after the vehicle had re-entered service with Walsall – and this trolleybus is being employed on the No. 15 route towards Blakenall.

(D. F. Parker)

Passing in Ingram Road during the rush hour are trolleybuses No. 855, (TDH 906), and No. 337, (NDH 954). The older vehicle is about to pull out in front of a parked Austin A90 'Hampshire'. No. 337, one of the Sunbeam F4s built with Brush H30/26R bodies in 1951, would not have been a regular performer on the Blakenall services because of its lower seating capacity. It is still wearing its original dark and light blue livery, while the large Sunbeam F4A 855 is in Edgley Cox's simplified all-over light blue with three very thin bands of yellow relief.

(D. R. Harvey Collection)

The trolleybuses leaving Ingram Road turned right into Field Road on their way back to Bloxwich on the 15 route. Here, Sunbeam F4A 857, (TDH 907), starts this manoeuvre when in the ownership of West Midlands PTE in the summer of 1970. This is why the trolleybus is not wearing the Walsall Corporation crests.

(R. Symons)

No. 851, (TDH 901), the former Commercial Motor Show exhibit of 1954, turns into Field Road from Ingram Road when travelling towards Bloxwich on the 15 service in about 1957. This end of the route was tree-lined with a mixture of former council houses and privately owned semi-detached housing dating from the 1920s. The trolleybus crew seem to be having a quiet time as their charge is virtually empty.

(D. R. Harvey Collection)

Walsall's only post-war, six-wheeled trolleybus, No. 350, (RDH 990), turns from Lichfield Road into Field Road when working on the 30 route from Bloxwich towards Blakenall. There were only forty-three of these Sunbeam S7s, all built between 1948 and 1950. Thirty went to Newcastle with Northern Coachbuilders bodywork and twelve went to Reading with Park Royal bodies and then there was RDH 990! If it was anything like the other examples of S7s, the steering on this trolleybus would have been very heavy and hard work for the driver. The Willowbrook body on this Metro-Vick 115hp-powered trolleybus was built as a PAYE vehicle with a seated conductor opposite the rear two-step back platform and a large area for fifteen standees in the same area. It was converted to a more conventional layout in February 1961 when it was renumbered from its original 850 to, as seen here, 350.

(J. Fozard)

No. 858, (TDH 908), another of the Willowbrook-bodied Sunbeam F4As is turning left from Field Road into Lichfield Road. The 15 and 30 routes shared the A4124 with the Lower Farm No. 32 service, which continued straight on for about a ¼ mile. The trolleybus is working on the No. 15 route back to Bloxwich, a journey that took, surprisingly, about six minutes.

(R. F. Mack)

On reaching Bloxwich the trolleybuses used Park Road to both leave and gain High Street, Bloxwich. With Bloxwich's Gothically-styled Victorian C of E School in the background, on 19 April 1969, two trolleybuses make the turn at Park Road. On the right is No. 338, (NDH 955), one of the Brush-bodied Sunbeam F4s of 1951, which is going to Walsall via Blakenall. Turning into High Street is No. 867, (XDH 67), a seventy-seater, Willowbrook-bodied Sunbeam F4A, which still has vestiges of the yellow livery bands beneath the lower saloon windows.

(P. J. Thompson)

Chapter Six

LOWER FARM

The Lower Farm Estate is a residential area, which stands to the north of Bloxwich and borders the rural land against the Staffordshire border. It was developed by the local council during the 1950s though most of the housing is now privately owned. In addition there are two multi-storey blocks of council flats on Lower Farm built in the 1960s.

The extension to the Lower Farm Estate was introduced on New Year's Eve 1962 at a time when much of the estate had yet to be completed. Numbered 32, the route was the penultimate Walsall trolleybus service to open. The route followed the 30 route to Bloxwich where it turned right at the northern end of Bloxwich's High Street into Park Road. It then turned right into Lichfield Road but whereas the circular 15 and 30 used the right turn into Field Road, the 32 continued along the A4124 to Little Bloxwich Bridge over the Wyrley & Essington Canal. This bridge was reconstructed and widened shortly after the introduction of the trolleybuses, during which time the trolleys operated on a single pair of overhead lines over the bridge. The 32 route then turned left into Stoney Lane where it descended into the heart of the compact Lower Farm Estate before turning right to its terminus in Buxton Road.

This short extension from Bloxwich along Lichfield Road into the 1950s housing estate was usually, though not exclusively, operated by the large capacity Sunbeam F4As.

Above: Turning from Park Road into the northern end of High Street, Bloxwich is a 1951-built four-wheeler. No. 336, (NDH 953), a Brush-bodied Sunbeam F4, is on its way back to Walsall from the Lower Farm Estate when working on the 32 route in about 1957. It would have taken the trolleybus some seven minutes to reach Bloxwich from Lower Farm. Just visible through the trees on the left is a Walsall Corporation Willowbrook-bodied motorbus. No. 336 is in its 'as delivered' livery of light blue with dark blue bands immediately above and below the lower saloon windows. There were two black bands below the upper saloon windows.

(W. J. Haynes)

Opposite, top: A later and more general view of the Park Road junction with High Street, shows Willowbrook-bodied Sunbeam F4A 853, (TDH 902), working into Bloxwich on the No. 32 route from Lower Farm. The low row of nineteenth-century cottages have long since been demolished, but the rest of this part of Bloxwich has changed very little in the interim years. Passing the trolleybus travelling in the opposite direction is a 1969-registered Austin Maxi. With a journey time from Lower Farm to Walsall of twenty-one minutes and a headway of an average of around thirty minutes the No. 32 route was worked in with the 15, 30, 31 and 33 services so that one could catch a Walsall-bound trolleybus every five to eight minutes.

(Travel Lens)

Below: Looking towards the Little Bloxwich Bridge over the Wyrley & Essington Canal in Lichfield Road, some 600yds away, trolleybus No. 872, (XDH 72), travels towards Bloxwich along Lichfield Road in the early 1960s. On the corner of Millfield Avenue on the left is the recently demolished Esso garage, while behind it is the Knave of Hearts public house, a typical 1950s-built public house which does survive at the time of writing. This trolleybus was the last of the batch and was the only one fitted with Lockheed Brakes and a Kirkstall back axle, resulting in a noisy differential and rather variable brakes.

(R. F. Mack)

Above: Travelling away from the 32 route terminus, No. 863 (TDH 913), a Sunbeam F4A, stands at the bus stop just before the shops on the corner of Fishley Lane. The trolleybus would continue straight on into Stoney Lane, which would take the trolleybus to the Lichfield Road junction near to the Beacon Way public house. Off to the right beyond the Ford Cortina are the only two multi-storey blocks of flat, Thomas House and Smith House, on the Lower Farm Estate.

(Travel Lens)

Opposite, top: The extended BUT 9611Ts were rarities on the Lower Farm Estate route. No. 876, (GFU 694), by now a forward-entrance, sixty-nine seater, is being used on a NTA trolleybus tour of the system on 3 October 1970, the final Saturday of operation. No. 876 is negotiating the traffic island at the junction of Buxton Road and Sanstone Road. The trolleybus had come from the Lichfield Road junction and descended Buxton Road where the telephone box is located.

(D. Johnson)

Below: Sitting at the Lower Farm Estate terminus of the 32 service is No. 864, (TDH 914). This Willowbrook-bodied Sunbeam F4A would be subsequently bought for preservation by the National Trolleybus Association, but that would be some years in the future. It is parked in front of the maisonettes in Buxton Road. The lightweight construction of these bodies was rather spoilt by the strange frontal design which ruined the otherwise standard Willowbrook body.

(J. Saunders)

Looking back across to the traffic island at the junction of Buxton Road and Sanstone Road where the trolleybus overhead turned back to the pick-up point, No. 863, (TDH 913), stands outside the 1960s maisonettes where the terminus was located. The trolleybus had by now lost its Walsall municipal crests showing that the trolleybus is operating during its last year of operation.

(Travel Lens)

CHAPTER SEVEN

MOSSLEY ESTATE

The development of the council-built housing estates in Beechdale, Dudley Fields and Mossley, in the Bloxwich area, to the north and the west of the Walsall, enabled a lot of sub-standard nineteenth-century housing to be replaced in the inner part of Walsall. Most of this residential development only began in the early post-war years after the farmland passed out of viable agricultural use at the edge of the existing urban area. Many of these Walsall housing estates are named after farms that had only survived into the first few years of peace because of the need to produce homegrown fresh produce as part of the war effort.

The Mossley estate north of Sneyd Lane dated from the later 1950s and became the third trolleybus route to be introduced under the Edgley Cox regime on 3 June 1957 as the 31 route. Again, it followed Bloxwich Road through Birchills and Leamore into Bloxwich. On arrival at the old Music Hall building it turned into Wolverhampton Road where it shared the wiring with the 33 circular service to Beechdale. Both routes used Bell Lane and Sneyd Lane. It then passed Sneyd Hall Road where the Walsall-bound 33 trolleybus route turned left, whereas the Mossley route continued for just over 200yds before reaching Cresswell Crescent where it turned right into the late 1950s-built Mossley Council Housing Estate. Initially it only went as far as Abbey Square but was extended to the Eagle public house on 20 September 1959.

This route was extensively photographed at the Eagle public house but not very much was taken between the entrance to the Mossley Estate and the Wolverhampton Road/ Bell Lane junction. Generally larger capacity buses were used on the service though other smaller types were drafted in when required.

On reaching Bloxwich, the 31 route turned left into Wolverhampton Road and headed towards the Bell Lane/Sneyd Lane junction. This road was used by both the Mossley and the Cavendish Road routes serving both the Dudley Fields and Beechdale housing estates. No. 860, (TDH 910), turns in front of Lawrence's cycle shop as it heads off to Mossley.

(J. S. Webb)

The section of Wolverhampton Road joining Bell Lane opposite the Sir Robert Peel public house was restricted to only buses and trolleybuses. No. 856, (TDH 906), a Willowbrook-bodied Sunbeam F4A, is about to pass between Davies House and, hidden by the trees on the right, Clarke House as it returns to Bloxwich on the 31 service from Mossley. After the closure of the trolleybus system this junction was closed to through traffic.

(J. Saunders)

Trolleybus 852, (TDH 902), turns off Bell Lane into Wolverhampton Road at the Sir Robert Peel public house, named after the founder of the police force (known as 'Peelers') who was twice Prime Minister and whose family had made its fortune in the nearby Fazeley textile industry. This Willowbrook-bodied Sunbeam F4A is working its way back to Bloxwich on the 31 route from Mossley in about 1966.

(R. F. Mack)

Above: Sunbeam F4A trolleybus No. 852, (TDH 902), has just crossed over the railway bridge in Sneyd Lane near to the site of the present-day Bloxwich railway station. This station, on the old South Staffordshire line between Walsall and Cannock, had been closed in 1963 and reopened under the auspices of Centro in 1989. The trolleybus, working on the 31 route, will continue past the left-hand turn into the Dudley Fields Estate taken by the 33 route and will travel further along Sneyd Lane until it turns right into Cresswell Crescent and into the Mossley Estate.

(D. R. Harvey Collection)

Opposite, top: Unloading in Cresswell Crescent is another 'Goldfish Bowl' trolleybus. This time No. 870, (XDH 70), one of the second batch of Sunbeam F4As, stands opposite the 1960s blocks of maisonettes with the row of 1920s semi-detached housing behind it in Sneyd Lane. The 31 route basically used Cresswell Crescent as a long cul-de-sac as its exit into Broad Lane virtually marked the Walsall-South Staffordshire boundary over which the trolleybuses could not cross.

(C. Carter)

Below: There was a row of shops in Cresswell Crescent within sight of Sneyd Lane which served the local community with its daily needs as well as providing a post office. Hidden by the trolleybus was the unusually named, M & B-owned Leathern Bottle public house. No. 864, (TDH 914), has left the terminus about ½ mile away and is heading towards Sneyd Lane. The lads in the upper saloon look towards the photographer with a mixture of curiosity and incredulity and hope that they can ruin the shot by waving or pulling a face.

(D. R. Harvey Collection)

Above: It was quite unusual for any of the small capacity trolleybuses to work on the 31 route as the service was normally operated by the large 70-seat Sunbeam F4As. Standing in the turning circle in front of The Eagle public house and almost at the junction with Broad Lane is 338, (NDH 955). This Sunbeam F4 dated from 1951 and, with the exception of the rebuilt front dome windows, its body was in surprisingly original condition.

(L. Mason)

Opposite, top: Another fairly unusual type of trolleybus to operate on the Mossley service was the trio of extended BUT 9611Ts. The Northern Coach Builders body had been built to the 1950 standard length of 26ft with a capacity of fifty-six seats. Now rebuilt to forward entrance and 30ft long with sixty-nine seats, No. 875, (GFU 693), was a good match for the standard Sunbeam F4As both in terms of its seating capacity and its performance. It is standing in the turning circle at The Eagle pub terminus.

(D. R. Harvey Collection)

Below: The original terminus of the Mossley route at Abbey Square was replaced when the route was extended to the Eagle Hotel in Cresswell Crescent, Mossley on 20 September 1959. Waiting at the terminus in 1970 is 866, (XDH 66), the solitary Willowbrook-bodied Sunbeam F4A to be converted to forward control. The staircase was moved to the front and the whole effect was very neat with the exception of the curious central rear emergency door.

(D. R. Harvey Collection)

CHAPTER EIGHT

CAVENDISH AVENUE

From the Townend area the main roads led to the west and north of the town. Wolverhampton Street led past the canal wharves on the Walsall Canal and on to the Wolverhampton Road. To the north is Green Lane that went the direct way towards Bloxwich and is now the main A34 road. This was the most direct route out of Walsall to Cannock.

The newly available land was within the existing Walsall boundary, and as soon as funds became available, huge areas of what had only recently been farmland was quickly developed. The need for public transport became important just at the time when the Corporation's general manager, R. Edgley Cox, was embarking on his trolleybus expansion scheme of the late 1950s, by which time Dudley Fields and parts of the other estates were completed and occupied.

Not only did the former agricultural land become turned over to housing, but in the Leamore Lane area, the development of new factory estates also took place in the late 1950s. This has resulted today in a thriving area of warehousing and light industry. Undoubtedly, the introduction of trolleybus services into these suburbs to the west of Bloxwich was a significant factor in the extension of the urban area landscape.

The Beechdale Estate route was given the route number 40 when it opened on 12 September 1955, although originally, and much to the chagrin of the local residents, the destination was shown as 'GIPSY LANE ESTATE'. The destination display was soon altered to 'BEECHDALE ESTATE' following numerous complaints. It left the Townend terminus opposite the former starting point of the 29 route at the top of Park Street by using a turning circle which took the trolleybuses into Green Lane. The area lying north of Blue Lane included maisonettes and multi-storey blocks of flats which were built in the earlier 1950s. North of Hospital Street, Green Lane became a heavily industrialised area with engineering works, tube works and a power station. After just over ¾ mile, the route turned left into Stevenson Avenue and immediately crossed the Wyrley & Essington Canal, which was still surrounded by heavy industry and derelict land. It was now in the Beechdale Estate where it originally terminated just north of Stephenson Square, the main shopping and community area of the Beechdale Estate, and turned around in a small clockwise loop.

On 1 November 1961, the service was extended through Leamore to Sneyd Hall Road, Dudley Fields and then following the 31 service back into Bloxwich. There it returned to the town centre by way of Bloxwich Road, thus forming another large circular service.

144

Yet, strictly speaking, it was not a circular service as the two town-centre termini were not linked, so the route was more like a horseshoe. A trolleybus leaving St Paul's Bus Station would, if it went all the way round the route, finish up at Townend Street, while a trolleybus leaving Townend Street would eventually reach journey's end in St Paul's Street. Unlike the Blakenall route with its separate route numbers for each direction, the Leamore service was just renumbered 33 wherever it went!

Confusingly, once the trolleybuses had reached the end of Stevenson Avenue coming from Walsall they turned *right* into Bloxwich Lane in front of Hatherton County Primary School towards Dudley Fields and Bloxwich on the 'circular' service. However, on 2 September 1963, a branch of the 33 route was built along Bloxwich Lane in the Beechdale Estate in the opposite direction to the junction with Cavendish Road in Leamore, marked in later years by the Magic Lantern public house. In theory, the No. 33 service to Cavendish Road was quite discrete from the 33 circular to Bloxwich, but there were cases when, on reaching Cavendish Road, the 33 trolleybuses proceeded to Bloxwich and not back to Walsall using the new lines erected in 1967.

There were intended to be two further extensions from this turning circle, one going back along Cavendish Road to Stevenson Avenue and the second being wired along the length of Bloxwich Lane to Anson Bridge in Bentley. The intention was to join with the Walsall-Wolverhampton joint service and create a route directly between Willenhall and Bloxwich. Unfortunately, the construction of the M6 motorway ended that proposal.

The apparently simple route along Green Lane to the Gipsy Lane Estate numbered 33 was eventually anything but simple by the time it became a circular service by way of Dudley Field, Bloxwich and back to St Paul's Bus Station. Firstly, it wasn't strictly speaking circular at all as there was no link between the two town termini. Secondly, the Bloxwich Lane extension to Cavendish Avenue meant that one of Walsall's most complex pieces of wiring had to be installed opposite Hatherton Junior & Infants School in Willenhall Lane for trips to and from Birchills depot.

Long before it was rebuilt into a forward entrance, trolleybus No. 866, (XDH 66), a Sunbeam MS2 with a seventy-seat Willowbrook body, is parked at the original 33 route terminus. The position of the trolley poles shows that this vehicle has come into the town via Green Lane and this was before the circular service via Bloxwich had been opened. Thus, the trolleybus is displaying the original destination display of 'BEECHDALE ESTATE 40'.

(R. F. Mack)

In almost as-bought condition, No. 305, (BDY 811), stands at the top of Park Street on 3 September 1960 outside Porritt's jewellery shop. The driver of the trolleybus has had the foresight to park this former Hastings Tramways vehicle with its front wheels already turned prior to making the near 180° turn and back to either Green Lane or Stafford Street. The destination boxes on these trolleybuses were not big enough to show the route number and so No. 305 is only displaying 'BEECHDALE ESTATE'.

(M. L. Comfort)

On the other side of the semi-circular Richmond's store was the entrance to Stafford Street that led to Bloxwich by way of Leamore. Displaying 'GIPSY LANE 40' on its destination blind, Willowbrook-bodied Sunbeam F4A trolleybus 862, (TDH 912), turns across the top of Park Street from its terminus and moves towards Green Lane where it will leave the town on its way towards the 1950s municipal housing estate in Stevenson Avenue. It was interesting that the Transport Department always spelt 'Gipsy' with an 'I' whereas it was spelt with a 'Y' by all the other sections of the council!

(W. J. Haynes)

Above: Turning across Townend from the Walsall town terminus on the left, with Park Street behind it, Sunbeam F4A 853, (TDH 903), is about to turn into Stafford Street in about 1966. It is working on the anti-clockwise 33 circular service via Stephenson Avenue and then on to the Cavendish Road turning circle in Bloxwich Lane. It would then return along Bloxwich Lane and continue via the Dudley Fields Estate to Bloxwich before returning to town along Green Lane.

(R. Symons)

Opposite, top: The inspector has marched purposefully to the cab door of Sunbeam F4A 867, (XDH 67), as it stands in Green Lane opposite the canopy of the ABC Cinema. It will shortly move across Townend to the terminus of the 33 route at the top of Park Street near to the distant Marsh & Baxter's pork butchers shop. These shops would soon be demolished, and for a time the trolleybuses would turn right into Townend Street where they terminated at the same stops previously used by the recently abandoned 29 joint service to Wolverhampton.

(R. Symons)

Below: When the Park Street terminus for the 33 route was closed in 1967, the 33 route coming into Walsall from Green Lane used the wiring around the back of the ABC Cinema in Townend Street and loaded at the shelters recently abandoned by the 29 trolleybus route to Wolverhampton. No. 861, (TDH 911), looking in dire need of a repaint, stands at the end shelter opposite the wholesale distribution depot of W. H. Smith. It will shortly move away to go back up Green Lane to serve the spur to Cavendish Road in Bloxwich Lane.

(D. Johnson)

Above: The confusing array of destinations exhibited by trolleybuses working on the No. 33 service is clearly displayed here. Showing 'CIRCULAR DUDLEY FIELDS ESTATE', No. 342, (NDH 959), the much rebuilt and extended Sunbeam F4 of 1951, has come from St Paul's Street and is travelling along Wisemore towards the turn into Stafford Street as it goes to Bloxwich and then on to the Dudley Fields Estate. The extent of the rebuilding of this trolleybus is best exemplified by the extra half-bay behind the front bulkhead and the white rubber mounts for the glazing.

(D. R. Harvey Collection)

Opposite, top: Having crossed Blue Lane West, Sunbeam F4A trolleybus No. 872, (XDH 72), travels on an outbound 33 service along Green Lane. On the opposite side of the road behind Kendrick's eight-wheeled Foden FG6 lorry is St Patrick's Roman Catholic church. The church was built on the corner site of Green Lane and Blue Lane East in 1965-6; this modern brown brick church was designed with dressings of blue brick and concrete.

(R. F. Mack)

Below: Coming into Walsall along Green Lane just north of Blue Lane is the seventy-seater Willowbrook-bodied Sunbeam F4A trolleybus No. 855, (TDH 905). It has come from Cavendish Road terminus in Bloxwich Lane on the 33 route. To the right of the trolleybus is the complex of eight-storey flats that replaced Victorian terraces in the late 1950s. One of the arguments put forward against trolleybuses was that they were route-bound and therefore unable to cope with the obstructions such as, in this case, road widening. No. 855 is somewhat putting that theory in considerable doubt!

(R. F. Mack)

Green Lane climbed gently towards Rayboulds Bridge once it had left behind the rows of Victorian terrace housing. Behind the trolleybus pictured are houses, already boarded up prior to demolition. This was the point where the urban landscape altered dramatically into one of heavy industry, with the cooling towers for the local Birchills Power Station towering over the small factory units; the power station was demolished in 1973. At this point, Green Lane runs parallel to the Wyrley & Essington Canal built in 1797 to serve the local brickworks and ironworks. The trolleybus, No. 857, (TDH 907), travels out of Walsall on its way to the Bloxwich Lane turning circle at the junction with Cavendish Road when working on the 33 route.

(D. R. Harvey Collection)

About to turn right into Upper Green Lane from Stevenson Avenue on its way back to Walsall is one of the large 1956-built Sunbeam F4A trolleybuses. No. 869, (XDH 69), is working on the No. 33 circular service back into Walsall at a time when most of the area was still largely awaiting redevelopment. Once the trolleybus had turned right it would cross over the former Midland Railway's Walsall to Wolverhampton Railway line, which was not particularly successful. Passenger services ceased in the 1930s but the line remained open as a goods route until 1966. This large Willowbrook-bodied, seventy seater had entered service on 1 September 1956 as part of the seven XDH-registered trolleybuses ordered to increase trolleybus frequencies and have a reserve ready for future route expansions.

(C. Carter)

Having left Upper Green Lane and turned into Stephenson Avenue, the trolleybuses immediately crossed the Wyrley & Essington Canal. Years earlier, this area had been covered by coal mines, brick works and iron foundries, but, by the late 1960s, most of this was derelict land and not redeveloped until the 1980s. Behind the Sunbeam F4A, trolleybus 855, (TDH 905), is the 1960s office block now occupied by the Homeserve Company.

(D. R. Harvey Collection)

'The King is Dead, Long live the King'. Two Edgley Cox-designed vehicles pass each other in Stephenson Avenue and both are equally idiosyncratic. The trolleybus is the ground-breaking Sunbeam F4A 851, (TDH 901), a seventy-seater that was exhibited at the 1954 Commercial Motor Show. With its somewhat unusual frontal appearance and weighing only 7 tons 5 cwt 2 qtrs, this lightweight construction Willowbrook-bodied trolleybus opened up the way for 30ft-long, two-axled, double-deck buses to operate in this country. Yet, eleven years later, Mr Cox had created a design for a bus that was, in the case of No. 41, (EDH 941C), only 28ft 6in long with two doors and the same seating capacity as the trolleybus. It was a Daimler 'Fleetline' CRG6LW with a Northern Counties body, which, from the front, could have been a trolleybus with a 'pusher' Diesel engine at the back.

(A. S. Bronn)

Above: The wide grassed open spaces on either side of Stephenson Avenue are well shown as one of the former Hastings Tramways trolleybuses 307, (BDY 813), a much re-glazed, Weymann-bodied Sunbeam W4 works on an enthusiast tour not long before it was withdrawn by WMPTE in February 1970. These trolleybuses were, after the closure of the Wolverhampton joint service, usually found on the Bloxwich or Lower Farm routes where their powerful 95hp motors could be used to their full advantage.

(D. R. Harvey Collection)

Opposite, top: Coming out of the original turning loop at Fleming Road in Stevenson Avenue is Willowbrook-bodied Sunbeam F4A 853, (TDH 903). By now numbered as part of the 33 route, this was the original terminus of the No. 40 route whose destination was 'Beechdale Estate'. Although used for shortworkings, after the route was extended to Bloxwich as a circular service in November 1961, this turning circle was not used more than a few times a day.

(R. F. Mack)

Below: Turning right into Stevenson Avenue from Bloxwich Lane from the 1963 extension to Cavendish Road is trolleybus No. 855, (TDH 905). The trolleybus is advertising the famous local nectar of Highgate Mild Beer. Above the trolleybus is a positive plethora of wiring which allowed a trolleybus travelling along either road in both directions. Behind the trolleybus is Hatherton Junior and Infants' School. The straight-on wiring along Bloxwich Lane was added in 1967. This was due to the introduction of the one-way system in the town centre when the Beechdale terminus was moved into Townend Street. This made depot workings a problem and this extra wiring in Bloxwich Lane made these journeys considerably easier.

(D. R. Harvey Collection)

Clattering through the overhead junction in Bloxwich Lane is another Sunbeam F4A. No. 869, (XDH 69), is travelling from Bloxwich on the No. 33 route and is passing the Hatherton Junior and Infants' School. It is going to the September 1963 extension to Cavendish Road, which was never extended to either of its intended destinations. This left the trolleybuses having to go to a dead-end trip of half a mile each way and then come back again before resuming their journey to either Walsall or Bloxwich. Behind the trolleybus are the 1960s-built factory and industrial units in Leamore Lane.

(R. Symons)

Even as late as 1969, after West Midlands PTE had taken over the operation of the Walsall trolleybus fleet, the terminus at Cavendish Road was still largely undeveloped with only the roads being laid out. In the distance are the cooling towers of the Birchills Power Station in Upper Green Lane. No. 338, (NDH 955), was one of the ten Brush-bodied Sunbeam F4s dating from 1951. The first five of the class had been withdrawn between 1966 and 1967 and while the rebuilt trolleybus No. 342 was bound to survive after the incurring of all the development costs, it was perhaps surprising that Nos. 338-341 would last until the closure of the system in October 1970. These four trolleybuses were at this time the oldest complete ones to be operating in England.

(D. Skevington)

Above: No. 866, (XDH 66), only ran for Walsall Corporation in its forward entrance guise for four months before the system was taken over by WMPTE. Freshly repainted and looking sparkling, the Willowbrook-bodied trolleybus stands in front of the then council-owned houses at the junction of Bloxwich Lane and on the right Cavendish Road. To the right on the as yet undeveloped land would be built the Magic Lantern public house.

(D. Johnson)

Opposite, top: The Co-operative electric milk float is parked in Bloxwich Lane outside the terraced 1960s council houses while the milkman is away doing his round. About to pass it, having just left the No. 33 terminus at the junction with Cavendish Road on its way back towards Stephenson Avenue, is Sunbeam F4A 867, (XDH 67). It is 28 March 1970 and the trolleybus has lost its municipal crests and is beginning to look a little unloved.

(J. H. Meredith)

Below: About to turn from Leamore Lane into Bloxwich Lane is No. 859, (TDH 909). It is travelling on the circular 33 service from Bloxwich and has passed through the Dudley Fields Estate. In the distance is the newly completed Frank F. Harrison Secondary School, but the rest of the land, designated for industrial use, has, at this time, yet to be built on. Despite the lack of building, the lady with the shopping basket who has just got off the trolleybus hadn't actually got that far to go before reaching the houses which face the oncoming trolleybus.

(C. Carter)

Above: The Dudley Fields municipal housing estate was built during the 1950s and in Sneyd Hall Road two blocks of shops were built. These had two-storey accommodation above the shops and included Dudley Fields Post Office, which is still there at the time of writing. The crew of the trolleybus walk back from the shops to their parked Willowbrook-bodied 869, (XDH 69), which is facing Central Drive. On the right is a group of prefabs on land that was subsequently part of an open space in the middle of the road.

(C. Carter)

Opposite, top: In the heart of the Dudley Fields Estate, Sneyd Hall Road had a large open space effectively forming a large central reservation. Yet another of the Willowbrook-bodied Sunbeam F4A trolleybuses, No. 854, (TDH 904), passes a Volkswagen Beetle as it travels along this section of the No. 33 route in about 1966. No. 854 had entered service on 4 March 1955, and of all the 63 F4As constructed the twenty-two Walsall ones were, with the exception of Belfast's 246, (2206 OI), the only 30ft-long versions of the model to be constructed.

(D. R. Harvey Collection)

Below: The overhead in Sneyd Lane, Bloxwich, shows that the Sunbeam F4A trolleybus working on the 33 route is approaching the left hand turn into Sneyd Hall Road. The overhead wires going straight on along Sneyd Lane are for the Mossley 31 route. Willowbrook-bodied 863, (TDH 913), has its trolleypoles already on the wires to take it left into the Dudley Fields Estate. It has crossed over the distant railway bridge on the former LNWR Cannock line which went through Bloxwich.

(C. Carter)

Travelling along Wolverhampton Road in Bloxwich on 7 July 1965, No. 863, (TDH 913), a Willowbrook-bodied, 30ft-long Sunbeam F4A trolleybus, is working on the 33 route to the Dudley Fields Estate. It has just left the distant High Street in Bloxwich and is passing Bloxwich Park as it goes towards Sneyd Lane. No. 863 had entered service in June 1955 just in time for the opening of the Blakenall Circular service, but these large trolleybuses were equally at home on this, the trolleybus route which meandered around the Beechdale Estate, as on the 'main-line' service directly to Bloxwich.

(H. F. Wheeller)

CHAPTER NINE

A MISCELLANY OF THIS AND THAT

NEW BUSES AND OFFICIAL PHOTOGRAPHS

The first Walsall trolleybus was going to be given the fleet number 7. Being tilt-tested to an angle of 28°, this English Electric-bodied AEC 663T is undertaking this rigorous procedure at the English Electric works in Preston in 1931. The trolleybus, displaying the destination 'WALSALL' for obvious reasons, would enter service as No. 151, (DH 8311), the first of the pair of AEC six-wheelers, hopefully without the dent on the nearside corner between the decks.

(D. R. Harvey Collection)

Going over to an impressive 32° is the second of the pair of Brush-bodied Guy BTXs. This was going to be numbered 10 but at the last minute it was renumbered 154, (DH 8314). The Brush staff must have been fairly confident that it would not topple over, as there are no 'visible means of support'!

(D. R. Harvey Collection)

Now there is a registration that would be expensive to purchase today! ADH 1 was the first of the five Beadle-bodied Sunbeams to be delivered in August 1933. The first of the Short- and Weymann-bodied examples were also delivered in the same month for driver training and familiarisation; these were Nos. 164, (ADH 10), and 167, (ADH 13), respectively. No. 155 has just been delivered as it is carrying a trade plate attached to the nearside headlight.

(Walsall Corporation)

Seen alongside ornamental balustrades on the Esplanade alongside the River Medway in Rochester on 29 September 1933 is No. 161, (ADH 7). This was the location where Short Brothers took all their official photographs between 1926 and 1936. This was the second of the five Sunbeam MS2s that were bodied by Short Brothers and clearly shows the two-step platform, the newly introduced cut-away at the rear of the entrance and the rather attractively-styled, rear emergency window.

(Short Brothers)

Even the chrome wheel centres sparkled as No. 166, (ADH 12), is posed for an official photograph just before it entered service on 1 October 1933. This was a Weymann-bodied Sunbeam MS2 and was a distinct improvement on earlier piano-front styled bodies that the Addlestone-based coachbuilder had produced. Yet while the rear styling of all these 1933-built trolleybuses looked really modern, the front end with its strangely stepped profile and dummy radiator grill still belonged to the period when body designers were still unsure of what to do with the cab area.

(Walsall Corporation)

Part of the line-up of brand new Sunbeam MS2 trolleybuses at Birchill's depot in 1933 shows Short-bodied 162 and 163, (ADH 8 and 9), on the right. Centre left is No. 166, (ADH 12), with its Weymann body, while on the left is No. 157, (ADH 3), a Beadle-bodied example. Although built to the same specification, the three body-builders' products clearly show subtle differences in the interpretation of the design.

(Walsall Corporation)

Even the body builders occasionally got it wrong as here some numerically dyslexic painter at the Park Royal factory managed to transpose the fleet numbers so that this vehicle is showing 178 on its front panel rather than the correct 187. This Park Royal-bodied Sunbeam MS2 was the first of the twins of 1938.

(Park Royal)

This Brush official photograph shows No. 334, (NDH 951), in all its glory. It has been prepared for exhibition at the 1950 Commercial Motor Show at Earl's Court. Looking extremely smart and with, no doubt, a 'special paint job', No. 334 would enter service on 19 December 1950, a full ten months before the remaining nine of the Walsall order would be delivered.

(Brush)

Mr Ronald Edgley Cox stands with other officials in front of the prototype Sunbeam F4A at the Willowbrook works in Loughborough in November 1954. No. 851, (XDH 901), seems to be rock steady on the tilt test frame at an angle of 28°. This was the minimum tilt for a double-decker, laden on the top deck with sand bags, to reach before it passed its Type Approval Certificate.

(Willowbrook)

Leading the Golden Jubilee Special line up of Walsall Corporation vehicles is Sunbeam F4A 851, (TDH 901). Behind it is motorbus No. 821, (TDH 73), a Daimler CVG5 with a lightweight Northern Counties body; No. 822 (TDH 769), the second ever lightweight AEC 'Regent' V MD3RV with a Park Royal body; and 823, (TDH 770), a Leyland 'Titan' PD2/20 with a lightweight Metro-Cammell 'Orion' body. The significance of this display for an open day at Birchills garage was that these four brand new vehicles had all appeared at the 1954 Commercial Motor Show.

(D. R. Harvey Collection)

The interior of the Willowbrook-bodied Sunbeam F4A 851 reveals a light and surprisingly airy interior, but also shows the single side panelling and the single-skinned roof interior. Also for such a long body there is a surprising lack of handrails and stanchions. This was all due to the desire to produce a lightweight body on what was normally a rather heavy trolleybus chassis. The result was a seventy-seat trolleybus with an all-up unladen weight of 7 tons 5 cwt 2 qtrs.

CHAPTER TEN

BIRCHILLS DEPOT

The large gabled offices of the Transport Department at Birchills garage in Bloxwich Road were built when the depot was opened by the South Staffordshire Tramways Company in June 1885 for the Bloxwich steam tram service. The South Staffs routes within the Borough were purchased, and on 1 January 1901 Birchills depot was acquired. The first twenty-eight trams were purchased in 1901 and the last ten cars, numbered 40-49, were purchased from Brush in 1920. The first buses were garaged at Birchills in 1915, but after using the old boiler house on the site. A new bus garage constructed in 1923 allowed all the vehicles to be housed under cover as well as having the facility to undertake all heavy repairs. Tramway replacement began in 1928 and the trolleybuses were parked in Road Five of the seven-road depot. The last Walsall trams ran on the Bloxwich route on 30 September 1933 when they were replaced by trolleybuses which took over part of the old tram sheds. By the outbreak of the Second World War the fleet numbered 157 motorbuses and 21 trolleybuses, all of which were garaged and maintained at Birchills. In the early hours of 31 July 1942, seven buses were destroyed in an air raid when incendiary bombs hit the garage. This was one of the last air raids to damage public transport in the West Midlands. The depot was expanded throughout the early post-war period and on the absorption of Walsall Corporation to West Midlands PTE, it became the largest bus garage in the North Division, while Walsall Works eventually became responsible for all of WMPTE and the later West Midlands Travel and Travel West Midlands bus overhauls and repaints.

This is a journey around the depot giving a flavour of what went on there in trolleybus days.

No. 154, (DH 8314), was the first of the pair of 1931-built Guy BTXs fitted with Brush five-bay bodies and unusual opening lower saloon windows in the cant rail panels as well as vertically sliding full-length windows in the upper saloon. The Guys had Rees-Roturbo 60hp motors with regenerative control but were somewhat underpowered. No. 154 is being re-poled in Birchills depot yard by a very strong-armed conductor! On the right, parked in the entrance to the tram depot, is tram No. 39, the last of the 1912-vintage seven UEC-bodied top-covered vestibuled trams, mounted on Brill 21E trucks. The trolleybus destination No. 28 was used on the joint service as a short working to Willenhall.

(R. T. Wilson)

Withdrawn but neatly parked at the rear of Birchills garage in 1946 is the 1931-built pair of AEC 663Ts 151 and 152, (DH8311-2), with English Electric H32/28R bodies on the right and the pair of Guy BTXs with Brush H32/28R bodies. All four trolleybuses were delivered for the opening of the Wolverhampton joint service but despite their orderly putting out to grass they would not be returned to service. The Guys were withdrawn in September 1945 while the AECs were both taken out of service on 17 February 1946, both pairs being replaced by 'Utility'-bodied Sunbeam W4s. All four still have the wartime blackout markings.

(R. A. Mills)

175

Formerly No. 163, No. 309, (ADH 9), a Short-bodied Sunbeam MS2 six-wheeler, is dumped at the rear of Birchills garage shortly after its withdrawal in September 1951. Behind it is No. 306, (ADH 6), the first of the same batch. The ten Beadle- and Brush-bodied MS2s of 1933 were all taken out of service when the ten NDH-registered Sunbeam F4s were placed into service. Judging by the condition of No. 309, with a good overhaul it looks as if it could have continued in use for a few more years.

(D. R. Harvey Collection)

Stripped and awaiting sale to the scrapman are two wartime trolleybuses and a Guy 'Arab' II bus, which had been withdrawn over three years earlier in November 1957! On the right, devoid of its outer rear tyres and some saloon glass, is the much rebuilt No. 323, (JDH 30). This was a Sunbeam W4 with a Park Royal body which dated from August 1943. Next to it is a similar, but nearly two years newer, 1945 vintage No. 328, (JDH 340), which seems to have survived in its original condition. Both of these trolleybuses were sold to Smith, Bilston in August 1961.

(A. D. Broughall)

Above: Standing at the entrance to Birchills depot is No. 333, (JDH 434). This was the last 'Utility'- bodied trolleybus to be purchased. This MV 95hp-motored Sunbeam W4 had a Roe H30/26R body and was delivered as fleet number 237 in March 1946. The front upper saloon windows have been rebuilt but otherwise the trolleybus is in original condition. It would remain in service until New Year's Eve 1965. Alongside it and behind it are two NDH-registered Brush-bodied Sunbeam F4s, although No. 337 has been repainted in the all-over light blue livery.

(D. R. Harvey Collection)

Opposite, top: Standing alongside the original tram sheds at Birchills is Brush-bodied Sunbeam F4 342, (NDH 959). Judging by the condition of the original two-tone blue paintwork, the bus is seen in the mid to late 1950s. These were the last trolleybus bodies to be built by Brush before it closed down its body-building activities and they were in essence a narrower version of the thirty F4s built in 1949 for Derby Corporation.

(R. F. Mack)

Below: This is what a trolleybus garage does best. Rows of neatly parked trolleybuses wait in Birchills garage with their trolleypoles on the wires but with their power switched off and the gear lever in neutral. Here one vehicle from each of the two batches of Willowbrook-bodied Sunbeam F4As, 864, (TDH 914), and 869, (XDH 69), stand in Birchills in 1969 awaiting their next day's duties.

(Travel Lens)

Above: This the sort of excellent work which Birchills works could achieve! Three of the four Grimsby-Cleethorpes Corporation Northern Counties-bodied BUT 9611Ts purchased in July 1960 were selected for extensive reconstruction. In the summer and autumn of that year, the former No. 164, (GFU 695), was transformed into a 30ft-long, sixty-seven-seater. Here, the original body stands behind its now lengthened chassis prior to its own lengthening. This trolleybus would go into Walsall service as No. 877, numerically their last in January 1962.

(J. Hughes Collection)

Opposite, top: The abandoned hulk of No. 873, (HBE 542), one of the pair of Crossley TDD42/3s with Roe H29/25R bodywork, stands in Birchills garage over the pits. It is a 'victim' of Edgley Cox's experiments! The gaping hole at the back is where the small Diesel oil engine was fitted, while what looks like a fuel tank is fitted between the wheelbase on the offside behind the bulkhead. This conversion work was begun early in 1968 and continued until work was stopped in January 1969, when Bournemouth's 300 was borrowed for further bi-modal surgery.

(D. R. Harvey Collection)

Below: Sunbeam MF2B 300, (300 LJ), was the trial trolleybus borrowed from Bournemouth Corporation with the intention of being rebuilt as the prototype for experiments with a rear-mounted oil-engine. The surviving thirty-eight MF2Bs were going to be purchased by Walsall in the early summer of 1969 in order to increase the size of the trolleybus fleet for the four proposed route extensions. With the impending formation of West Midland PTE, neither the new routes or the purchase of the trolleybuses from Bournemouth took place. Similarly, the conversion work at the rear end of 300 was suspended and is it is seen here unceremonially dumped at Wombwell Diesels in company with Birmingham City Transport 2185, (JOJ 185), early in 1970. What a near miss!

(D. R. Harvey Collection)

In February 1970, the first tranche of former Walsall trolleybuses withdrawn by WMPTE stands in the snow at the rear of Birchills garage. The three identifiable former Hastings Sunbeam W4s are 309, 307 and 306 with the solitary un-rebuilt BUT 9611T 874, (GFU 692), facing the railings, while against the garage wall is former Ipswich 344 (ADX 193). All of these trolleybuses were sold in May 1970 to Wombwell Diesels for scrap.

(D. R. Harvey Collection)

Before regulations prevented it, Land Rovers were a valuable member of many a service fleet and were frequently used to tow buses. This was for many years the norm in Walsall. VDH 573 was a long-wheelbase Land Rover and was in the fleet between July 1955 and 1960. It is retrieving the broken-down Sunbeam F4 trolleybus No. 342 on a rigid bar tow.

(S. N. J. White)

A vital part of the service fleet of any trolleybus operator was the tower wagon. Walsall had eight motorised tower wagons between 1912 and the closure of the system and 706 BDH was the sixth one. The tower wagons were used for overhead line erection, removal and maintenance and to come out to assist trolleybuses that had their trolley poles damaged. This Karrier Gamecock was fitted with a Willowbrook-built crew-cab. It entered service in December 1957 and eventually survived with WMPTE until 1975.

(D. R. Harvey Collection)

Chapter Eleven

THE FINAL MISCELLANY

Standing in front of the four-month-old trolleybus No. 226, (JDH 30), is the first group of Walsall Corporation's female trolleybus drivers. The driving instructor looks a little apprehensive as he stands with three smiling women on each side of him who are shortly to be let loose on driving duties. Female tram conductresses were employed during the Great War but were soon dismissed when the men returned from the Armed Forces. In the Second World War, manpower was again reduced as men were called up. For some operators the size of the work force became so critically low that once again women were employed as in this case actually to drive the trolleybuses. Sunday 12 December 1943 looks as if it was a bitterly cold day as Miss P. N. Thomas stands on the left with the other five new female drivers.

(Walsall Corporation)

The first of the 1933-vintage trolleybuses to be withdrawn was 303, (ADH 3), which went in January 1951. It was converted into the Walsall Festival of Britain illuminated float and toured the roads on which trolleybuses could run, which realistically was only on the Bloxwich Road and as far as Willenhall on the joint service. Festooned with fairy lights the trolleybus stands in Birchills yard and is using the trade plate 038 DH.

(R. Smith)

Wolverhampton Trolleybus Group undertook a tour of the Walsall and Wolverhampton systems and used a freshly overhauled Sunbeam F4A for the purpose *(see page 186)*. It meant that this large seventy-seater went to parts of the Wolverhampton system where a Walsall trolleybus was unlikely ever to have gone before or afterwards! No. 869, (XDH 69), speeds along Priory Street in Dudley as it travels the short distance to the terminus outside the impressive Regency frontage of the Saracen's Head and Freemason's Arms public house in Stone Street. At this time Priory Street was a two-way road but today traffic can only pass towards the distant Wolverhampton Street, which was the original Wolverhampton & District tram terminus.

(J. Hughes Collection)

In September 1955, No. 864, (TDH 914), was demonstrated around the Portsmouth Passenger Transport Department's trolleybus system. This was not only demonstrating for the undertaking who employed No. 864 on a number of their services but also for the benefit of the general managers who were attending the annual conference for the Municipal Passenger Transport Association. No. 864 stands at the South Parade Pier when working on Portsmouth's No. 6 trolleybus service.

(D. A. Jones)

The picture says it all!
THE END.

(D. Johnson)

WALSALL TROLLEYBUS SYSTEM MAP

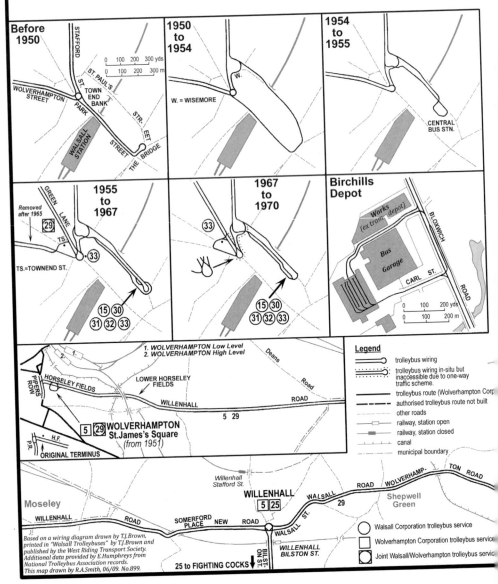

WALSALL CORPORATION TRANSPORT
Trolleybus Wiring - 1965

Before 1950

1950 to 1954

1954 to 1955

1955 to 1967

1967 to 1970

Birchills Depot

W. = WISEMORE

Removed after 1965

TS.=TOWNEND ST.

CENTRAL BUS STN.

Works (ex tram depot)

Bus Garage

1. WOLVERHAMPTON Low Level
2. WOLVERHAMPTON High Level

HORSELEY FIELDS

LOWER HORSELEY FIELDS

WILLENHALL ROAD

5 29

WOLVERHAMPTON St.James's Square
(from 1951)

ORIGINAL TERMINUS

Legend

- trolleybus wiring
- trolleybus wiring in-situ but inaccessible due to one-way traffic scheme.
- trolleybus route (Wolverhampton Corp
- authorised trolleybus route not built
- other roads
- railway, station open
- railway, station closed
- canal
- municipal boundary

Moseley

Willenhall Stafford St.

WILLENHALL

SOMERFORD PLACE   NEW ROAD

WILLENHALL ROAD

WILLENHALL BILSTON ST.

25 to FIGHTING COCKS

WALSALL ROAD   WOLVERHAMP- TON ROAD

Shepwell Green

○ Walsall Corporation trolleybus service

□ Wolverhampton Corporation trolleybus service

◻ Joint Walsall/Wolverhampton trolleybus service

Based on a wiring diagram drawn by T.J.Brown, printed in "Walsall Trolleybuses" by T.J.Brown and published by the West Riding Transport Society. Additional data provided by E.Humphreys from National Trolleybus Association records. This map drawn by R.A.Smith, 06/09. No.899.

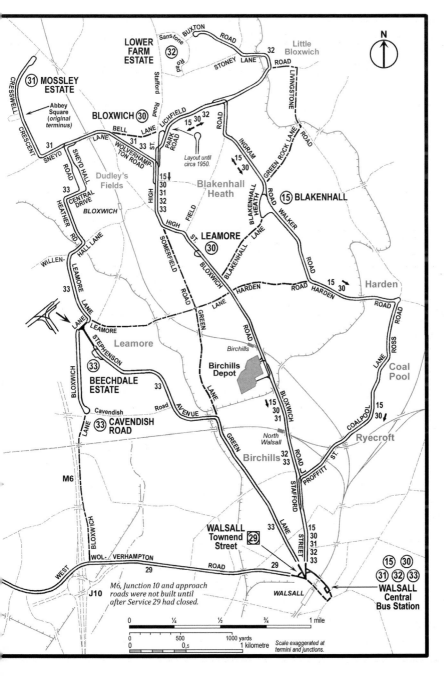

N

LOWER FARM ESTATE ③②

Little Bloxwich

Sandstone Road
BUXTON ROAD
STONEY LANE
Road
32
32

LIVINGSTONE ROAD

③① MOSSLEY ESTATE

CRESSWELL

Abbey Square (original terminus)

BLOXWICH ③⓪

BELL LANE
LICHFIELD ST.
PARK ROAD
15 30 32

GREEN ROCK LANE ROAD

Stafford Road

CRESCENT

31

SNEYD

Road

SNEYD HALL ROAD

WOLVERHAMP-TON ROAD

31

33

Layout until circa 1950.

INGRAM ROAD

15
30

33

HEATHER RD.

CENTRAL DRIVE

Dudley's Fields

15
30
31
32
33

Blakenhall Heath

HIGH

BLAKENHALL HEATH ROAD

⑮ BLAKENHALL

BLOXWICH

WALKER ROAD

HALL LANE

WILLEN-

LEAMORE LANE

HIGH ST.

LEAMORE ③⓪

BLAKENHALL LANE

33

SOMERFIELD ROAD

BLOXWICH ROAD

Road

15
30

Harden

HARDEN LANE

GREEN ROAD

HARDEN ROAD

HARDEN ROAD

ROSS ROAD

LEAMORE LANE

STEPHENSON

Leamore

Birchills

Birchills Depot

Coal Pool

BLOXWICH LANE

③③

BEECHDALE ESTATE

33

COALPOOL LANE

15
30

Cavendish Road

AVENUE

③③ CAVENDISH ROAD

GREEN LANE

15
30
31

BLOXWICH ROAD

Ryecroft

North Walsall

M6

Birchills

32
33

STAFFORD ROAD

PROFFITT ST.

BLOXWICH ROAD

WEST

WOL-VERHAMPTON ROAD

WALSALL Townend Street ㉙

33

GREEN LANE

STREET

15
30
31
32
33

⑮ ③⓪
③① ③② ③③

WALSALL Central Bus Station

J10

M6, Junction 10 and approach roads were not built until after Service 29 had closed.

29

29

WALSALL

0   ¼   ½   ¾   1 mile
0   500   1000 yards
0   0,5   1 kilometre

Scale exaggerated at termini and junctions.

ACKNOWLEDGEMENTS

When Walsall's trolleybuses went onto the town's streets it became the thirty-second system to open in the United Kingdom. The closure of the system in October 1970 only left two other systems at Teesside and Bradford operating. The contrast between the small number of official photographs taken at the opening of the Willenhall route and the amount of film taken on the final day of operation was enormous. This rather reflected the way the system was photographed, with a trickle of early material rising to a crescendo at the end. The late J.S. Webb and the late R. Wilson, who both came from Walsall, each took a number of photographs during the war and in the 1950s but many of their negatives have unfortunately disappeared. The result is a tantalising glimpse of some of their pictures taken on poor quality film, which although of historical importance often is of only an adequate standard.

All the other photographers are acknowledged, where known, in the text otherwise they are credited to my own collection. I sincerely thank all of those who are still alive for allowing me to use pictures, many of which were taken more than forty-five years ago.

I would also wish to thank John Hughes and Jason Matthews for both proof reading and providing me with information and to Rob Bentley and Jim Laws who located through CaMRA, the names and histories of several long disappeared land mark public houses. Steven Lockwood helped me to find book for research purposes and Bob Rowe, an author of a future publication about Walsall and I exchanged a number of pieces of factual information. A big thanks is due to Roger Smith for drawing yet another of his wonderful maps. Finally, I would like to thank my long-suffering wife, Diana, who has proof-read the whole manuscript.

David Harvey, June 2009